S0-BCY-867

MANY SERVANTS

An Introduction to Deacons

Ormonde Plater

COWLEY PUBLICATIONS

Cambridge ✦ Boston
Massachusetts

BV
680
.P55
1991

© 1991 Ormonde Plater
All rights reserved.

Published in the United States of America
by Cowley Publications, a division of the Society of St. John
the Evangelist. No portion of this book may be reproduced, stored in
or introduced into a retrieval system, or transmitted, in any form or
by any means, including photocopying, without the prior written permission of Cowley Publications, except in the case of brief
quotations embodied in critical articles and reviews.

International Standard Book Number: 1-56101-043-X
Library of Congress Number: 91-622

Library of Congress Cataloging-in-Publication Data
Plater, Ormonde.
Many servants : an introduction to deacons / Ormonde Plater.
p. cm.
Includes bibliographical references and index.
ISBN 1-56101-043-X
Deacons. I. Title.
BV680.P55 1991
262'.14—DC20   91-622

This book is printed on acid-free paper and was produced in the
United States of America.

Cowley Publications
28 Temple Place
Boston, Massachusetts 02111

Acknowledgments

Many persons have helped me write this book. James M. Barnett shared his views on the early diaconate. Sister Teresa, a deacon of the Community of St. Andrew in England, contributed insights about the early church, women deacons, and the Anglican communion, Owanah Anderson about native American deacons, and Sandra H. Boyd about early deaconesses. Josephine Borgeson and Edwin F. Hallenbeck, deacons involved in the contemporary revival, helped to clarify events in the Episcopal Church, and Constantino J. Ferriola did the same for Roman Catholic deacons. Many deacons told me their stories, and many other persons provided details about deacons in their dioceses. H. Boone Porter and William H. Petersen read the manuscript with careful and scholarly attention. Every writer should have an editor as competent as Cynthia Shattuck of Cowley Publications. My wife Kay read each chapter as it emerged, suggested corrections, and gave love without which I could not have proceeded.

Scriptural quotations are from the *New Revised Standard Version* (1990), while psalms are quoted from the Book of Common Prayer of the Episcopal Church.

C owley Publications is a ministry of the Society of St. John the Evangelist, a religious community for men in the Episcopal Church. Emerging from the Society's tradition of prayer, theological reflection, and diversity of mission, the press is centered in the rich heritage of the Anglican Communion.

Cowley Publications seeks to provide books, audio cassettes, and other resources for the ongoing theological exploration and spiritual development of the Episcopal Church and others in the body of Christ. To this end, it is dedicated to developing a new generation of theological writers, encouraging them to produce timely, creative, and stimulating publications of excellence, and making these publications available widely, reaching both clergy and lay persons.

Contents

Introduction

*T*his book is my attempt to tell the story of the deacons of the church. Among many forms of religious renewal, in the last two decades, Christian churches have experienced the recovery of the order of deacons after centuries of neglect and misuse. Once perceived as partially formed clerics growing toward the complete priesthood, or as liturgical assistants, deacons now appear in many places in a fully mature role as persons specifically chosen and committed for life to a work of ordained service. Although this book is mainly about the deacons of the American Episcopal Church, the renewal of the diaconate plays an important role in the Roman Catholic Church, in Lutheran and other reformed churches, in Orthodoxy, and in ecumenical endeavors at the national and international levels.

In all churches that have recovered the diaconate, the work has involved efforts to determine the meaning and functions of the order, and its relationship to other orders and forms of ministry, based on its origins in Scripture, its unfolding and evolution in the early church, and its re-emergence in recent times. In this recovery no motivation has been more influential than the biblical concept of *diakonia*, commonly defined as service, especially charity or care of the needy, derived from the ancient responsibility of all Jews and Christians to serve other persons and fortified by the urgent need for such service in our own age. A significant interest in social care arose in Europe in the early nineteenth century, a continent afflicted by war and poverty, and continued into this century. In our time, in a world even more devastated and unstable, one attribute of all Christian churches has been a concern to care for the needs of the world outside. Churches that once served mainly their own members have learned again to serve others. In every diocese, every parish and mission, through church, ecumenical, and secular organizations, as members of groups and as individuals, at work and at home, Christians are reaching out to those in need. In this renewal they bring to life an ancient Hebrew and Christian tradition: mercy, peace, and justice for the poor of Yahweh and Jesus.

Since about 1980, most deacons in the Episcopal Church have become closely identified with the baptismal ministry of ordinary Christian people who reach out to the poor, sick, and oppressed. Although care of the needy has thus become established as the main work of deacons, attempts to restore the order have caused controversy, debate, and resistance in some places. If care of the poor is the common obligation of every Christian, why bother to ordain deacons to do this same work? It is not enough, apparently, to appeal to Scripture and ancient tradition for the meaning and role of the order, or to point out that the liturgy of the church includes deacons as a full and equal order. Attempts to answer questions about the necessity of a real and vibrant diaconate have involved two main approaches, both based on the diaconate as it existed in the early church. First, as distinct symbols of Christ the Servant, deacons function among the faithful as special models of common Christian service who lead, enable, and encourage other Christians in charitable service. Second, the functions of deacons extend beyond the ordinary charitable work of all Christians into areas where official sanction, lifelong commitment, and sacramental grace are thought to strengthen the activity of the church. Many deacons serve in administrative positions, often within the diocesan structure, and deacons in general take seriously the bishop's command at their ordination to interpret the world to the church. Recent scholarly study, challenging the currently popular translation of the Greek word *diakonia* and its cognates as "service" and the like, especially in the sense of menial labor, tends to support this expansion in the ministry of deacons.

These two approaches are not without their own problems. One is the ambiguous meaning of *symbol* in the world today. In earlier centuries the symbols or sacramental signs of the church, including its ordained ministry, were supposed to be elevated, distant, somewhat inaccessible, and clearly defined. Although this attitude has not entirely disappeared, we now live in a society in which most people prize function for its practicality, and tend to ignore or disparage symbols for their inefficiency, playfulness, and uncertain effect on the emotions. In the popular mind, if it's just a symbol, to hell with it! In this mentality ministry has become reduced to the performance of necessary ecclesial tasks, for which ordination is less an essential than training and competency. Since priests and other baptized persons between them can perform all the liturgical, pastoral, and social tasks of deacons, a diaconate defined in terms of symbol makes little practical sense to many persons. Moreover, the diaconate appears to complicate, and to clutter with an additional dose of clericalism, a church that is trying to restore the ministry of all the baptized.

All ministry in the church—not just the ordained—is undergoing drastic change and appears to be heading for an unpredictable future. This is especially true of the diaconate, which tends to avoid not only a fixed definition but also a fixed place in the church. Deacons continually explore their origins, try new directions, and test the limits of their ministry. They like to speak of themselves as occupying some vague space between church and world, or between clergy and laity, as a bridge or as dancers on a razor's edge, whereas many others in the leadership of the church prefer to cling to established roles with distinct duties and responsibilities. Those who prefer simple meanings, rigid structures, and clear answers will not find them in the modern diaconate, which seems always in the process of becoming something else with other meanings and other functions. Dioceses and parishes that encourage deacons to evolve and change in their ministry, and that allow free rein to local imagination and creativity, seem to have the least difficulty with problems of definition and role.

Another problem concerns a fundamental contradiction in the way the church uses the order. To renew the diaconate, we have had to take a medieval practice—the deacon as temporary intern for priest—and alongside it reestablish an ancient practice—the deacon as permanent servant of the church. The two forms of the diaconate, ancient and medieval, carry the same name and are entered through the same ordination rite, but they are by no means equivalent, and they coexist in an uneasy parallel. The restoration of the ancient practice of the diaconate has resulted in differences between deacons and priests (including transitional deacons on the way to the priesthood) in status, lifestyle, and ministry. As with all reform, these distinctions have produced confusion, anger, and resistance—among lay persons who view deacons as a threat to their baptismal ministry, among priests who cherish the diaconate into which they were once received, and even among those deacons who identify themselves closely with the priesthood. The restoration of the diaconate challenges the church to find new ways of expressing the ancient bond of service between deacons and bishops, and to develop a healthy relationship among deacons, priests, and other Christian ministers based on a theology of mutual and distinct ministry, not on practices that nourish disorder and competition.

Even in places where the order has been successfully restored, it tends to evolve in unexpected ways, creating new and often surprising forms of an ancient order. Changes in the diaconate tend to change the church. Ultimately, the only answer to the problem of change is to allow the change to take place, to observe what happens, and to share the story.

The design of this book, then, is to reflect on the history of service and servants in the church, and to record the emerging meanings and functions of *diakonia* and deacons in the modern church and the directions in which they appear to be heading. Many dioceses of the Episcopal Church select, form, deploy, and supervise and support deacons. Some dioceses of the Anglican Church of Canada are joining this renewal, and other churches are observing the Anglican experience for help in their own efforts. Thus another purpose of this book is to provide information and guidance for the revival of the diaconate.

The late Wesley Frensdorff told me some years ago about an old Yiddish curse: "May you have many servants!" The curse has in mind those servants who are lazy afflictions; they corrupt the house with lewdness and theft, and bind their master and mistress in chains of disorder. In this book I extol the virtues of good servants, as articulate and cheerful as Figaro and Susanna, as resourceful and intelligent as Jeeves, as loyal and energetic as Bunter, as strong and enduring as Dilsey, and argue that God will provide good servants to those

who seek them and sustain them. Good servants free
those they serve, and many good servants free many.

1

Origins

S ayings and stories about servants constitute a major ingredient of Scripture. In the ancient writings of the Hebrew people, themes of mercy and justice are prominent, and in the Christian writings, which contain several references to early deacons, Jesus and his followers teach love of others and perform acts of compassion. This scriptural basis has reinforced the modern understanding of the diaconate as a ministry of social care, as a sacramental representation of the servant Christ and his serving church, and as part of God's ordering of the church in a divine plan of creation and salvation.

The Hebrew scriptures

The biblical tradition of charity is older than the Torah, older than even the Hebrew people, and broader in ethnic scope.[1] The desire to help the oppressed and dispossessed is so primitive and widespread that we may assume service for the benefit of others is a natural tendency in the human race. Over countless ages human beings have inherited and absorbed the practice of caring for others. By the design of God we are born to service, with good fortune we learn service in the hospitality of our first home, and at our best we hand over service to the young, who do the same in their turn. Our natural inclination to serve God and each other comes from our nature as creatures made in the image of God.

In the older, Yahwist account of creation, the first activity of Adam is to till and keep the garden of Eden (Gen 2:15). In a myth passed on by oral tradition and finally written down, Adam begins existence as a farmhand of the Lord. Even when he falls, and is sent forth from Eden, his work is "to till the ground from which he was taken" (Gen 3:23). In the account of the great flood Noah gathers and keeps animals and feeds them (Gen 7). He is a livestock servant of the Lord. These myths consistently place human beings in a relationship to God.

Our relationship to God inspires our relationship to our neighbor, service for the benefit of other people. A particular concern of ancient Near Eastern legal codes is relief of the suffering of the poor, widows and orphans, aliens, and the oppressed. This concern carries over into the legal collections of the Old Testament, which were descended from ancient case law. The major legal collections of the Torah or Pentateuch show consistent concern for the poor, or *anawim*, a term which includes all those in need. In all of the collections the people of God are commanded to treat the poor with charity and justice, and this concern is linked with regulations for worship.

The earliest of these is the Covenant Code (Ex 20:22 – 23:33), and among its many cultic regulations and laws protecting human beings and property are prohibitions against wronging aliens, widows and orphans, the poor, and others in need (Ex 22:21-26; 23:1-9). The central episode of Israel as the people of God includes their experience as slaves in Egypt, saved through the mercy and justice of God. Thus, when the Covenant Code forbids the listener to wrong and oppress a stranger, it adds: "you know the heart of an alien, for you were aliens in the land of Egypt" (Ex 23:9). This refrain appears also in the later codes.

The Deuteronomic Code (Deut 12-26), believed to be the famous scroll, or Book of the Law, "discovered" in the temple in 621 BCE, stresses justice, equity, care of the poor, and hospitality for the sojourner (or resident alien): "When you reap your harvest in your field and forget a sheaf in the field, you shall not go back to get it; it shall be left for the alien, the orphan, and the widow" (24:19). And the reason for the command: "Remember that you were a slave in the land of Egypt" (24:22). The law proves sensitive even to ecology: "If you come on a bird's nest, in any tree or on the ground, with fledglings or eggs, with the mother sitting on the fledglings or on the eggs, you shall not take the mother with the young" (22:6).

Finally, the Holiness Code (Lev 17-26) contains mainly religious and cultic laws. Israel must be holy as God is holy. But in one section, chapter 19, the code groups commands that are primarily ethical, in the tradition of the Decalogue, the Covenant Code, and the Deuteronomic Code. Gleanings from fields and vineyards shall be left "for the poor and the alien" (19:10); "When an alien resides with you in your land, you shall not oppress the alien" (19:33). And again the reason: "for you were aliens in the land of Egypt" (19:34).

In all of these collections, the memory of the Exodus informs the Hebrew understanding of humanitarian needs and concerns. Yet the Hebrew experience and remembrance of salvation also include the profound knowledge that God is the source and example of mercy. Justice is the beginning and goal of ritual. Service of the poor embraces service of the Lord. Praise of God includes praise of the Lord who uplifts the poor:

> For the Lord your God is God of gods and Lord of lords, the great God, mighty and awesome, who is not partial and takes no bribes, who executes justice for the or-

phan and the widow, and who loves the strangers, providing them food and clothing. You shall also love the stranger, for you were strangers in the land of Egypt. [Deut 10:17-19]

Justice for the poor persists as a major theme in other Hebrew writings. In the Song of Hannah (1 Sam 2:1-10) she praises the Lord who "raises up the poor from the dust" and "lifts the needy from the ash heap, to make them sit with princes and inherit a seat of honor." Hannah's prayer is the model for the Song of Mary (Magnificat) in Luke; both songs speak about God's power to raise the downtrodden. Hannah prays to the Lord as his "servant" (1:11) and conceives Samuel, who is consecrated to the service of the Lord.

Justice for the *anawim* is also a prominent theme in many psalms. Whatever the tangled history of their date and authorship, the psalms, once attributed to David, represent the heart of Hebrew worship. There the God who brought Israel out of Egypt is "the helper of orphans" (Ps 10:15), who "does not despise nor abhor the poor in their poverty" (Ps 22:23), and who will set right the victims of crooked deeds. The law is the subject of the extended meditation of Psalm 119, in which righteousness is defined as service of the Lord according to his commandments. Another prominent theme of the psalms is praise of the Lord who helps the poor. Psalm 146 sings of God

> Who gives justice to those who are oppressed,*
> and food to those who hunger.
> The Lord sets the prisoners free;
> the Lord opens the eyes of the blind;*
> the Lord lifts up those who are bowed down.
> The Lord loves the righteous;
> the Lord cares for the stranger;*
> he sustains the orphan and widow,
> but frustrates the way of the wicked. [Ps 146:6-8]

This passage, important in prophetic literature, appears in slightly different form in Isaiah 61:1-2, which Jesus reads in the synagogue at Nazareth:

> The Spirit of the Lord is upon me,
> because he has anointed me
> to bring good news to the poor.
> He has sent me to proclaim release to the captives
> and recovery of sight to the blind,
> to let the oppressed go free,
> to proclaim the year of the Lord's favor. [Lk 4:18-19]

Concern for the poor is also a major message of the prophets. A prophet, a *nabi*, is also an advocate, a *goel*, who speaks for God as a voice for the voiceless. Amos, Hosea, Micah, and Isaiah attack the corruption and injustice typical of both kingdoms in the eighth century, and the prophets just before and during the exile in Babylon continue the old theme. In the Temple Sermon, Jeremiah ascribes God's protection not to the presence of the temple but to the morality of the people:

> For if you truly amend your ways and your doings, if you truly act justly one with another, if you do not oppress the alien, the orphan, and the widow, or shed innocent blood in this place, and if you do not go after other gods to your own hurt, then I will dwell with you in this place, in the land that I gave of old to your ancestors forever and ever. [Jer 7:5-7]

The temple was built to house the commandments, but the people forgot to obey the commandments, especially those to ensure justice and true worship. The great prophet of the Exile, Ezekiel, defines righteousness as individual deeds of justice. The righteous one "does not oppress anyone, but restores to the debtor his pledge, commits no robbery, gives his bread to the hungry and covers the naked with a garment, does not take advance or accrued interest" (18:7-8). Ezekiel's famous vision in which the spirit of God enters the dry bones of the exiles while sinews and flesh grow upon them (37:1-14) must be interpreted as a people restored not only to a place, but also to deeds of justice.

From the earliest legal collections to the prophetic writings after the Exile, therefore, the Hebrew scriptures are consistent in their moral teachings about care for the poor. Among the poor (*anawim*) they number all the afflicted, especially the powerless and the oppressed, the humble and meek, widows and orphans, and "strangers" (sojourners and aliens). All these categories of the poor remind the Hebrew people not only of their ancient history as slaves and outcasts, but also of their obligation to help the poor always.

Biblical references to servants are varied and often confusing in meaning. A common word in the Hebrew scriptures is the noun *'ebed*, which means servant (in a number of senses) but also household slave, child, subject of a king, and worshiper of God. In the Septuagint, the Hebrew scriptures of Hellenistic Jews and Christians, *'ebed* is never translated *diakonos* (minister or servant) but *doulos* (slave) or *pais* (child). Although many early Christians appear to have emphasized the latter meanings, the most common interpretation today is servant. Of all the many meanings of this term and its cognates, however, its cultic or liturgical aspect has been the most neglected. The purpose of the exodus from Egypt is not solely freedom from slavery, for God saves the people of Israel out of Egypt to render *'abodah*, or worshipful service, to Yahweh. This is the context, a fundamental affinity with God, in which servants perform compassion. Out of their sacrifices of blood and incense, of praise and thanksgiving, flow works of mercy and justice.

Most uses of *'ebed* involve a common or ordinary use of servant imagery, applied to God's creation, to men and women made in the image of God, and to God's chosen people. But there is also a specific, theologically heightened dimension—the *'ebed Yahweh*, or servant of the Lord. The *'ebed Yahweh* is a specially designated person, a servant *of* the Lord but also united *with* the Lord, carrying out God's commandments and God's plan of creation and salvation. In the Hebrew scriptures this servant acts as divine agent principally in the prophecies of Second Isaiah (Isa 40-55), and most importantly in the great Servant Songs, written in joyful hope of the restoration from exile in Babylon. For the author of the songs, *'ebed Yahweh* appears to be the nation of Israel, chosen by God, suffering in exile, ultimately faithful, and restored out of death. For Christians, Isaiah's portrayal of the suffering servant of the Lord constitutes the most explicit prophecy in the Hebrew scriptures of the incarnation, death, and resurrection of Jesus. The songs live on in the gospel when Jesus says that he came not to be served but to serve. He is the servant whom the Lord has chosen to save the people of God. The church, the image of Christ, is the body which makes the servant of the Lord present among us, and the deacons, the servants of the church, continually remind the people of the image of service in Christ.

The Christian scriptures

When we turn to the New Testament, the tradition that we found in the Hebrew writings abounds in the teachings and deeds of Jesus as well as in the stories, sayings, and writings of early Christians.[2] The biblical tradition is commonly identified with the teaching of Christ that "whoever wishes to become great among you must be your servant, and whoever wishes to be first among you must be slave of all," and with the description of Christ as one who "came not to be served but to serve, and to give his life as a ransom for many" (Mk 10:43-45). This passage and related ones are widely used today to depict Christ as the model for the service of all baptized Christians, as well as for the deacons who serve in a special way. When the passage is taken in its entirety, however, the *diakonia* that Christ came to render seems to be not care of the needy but death on the cross.

There is no question that care of the needy is a Christian imperative. When he is challenged to justify his actions on the basis of the law, Jesus summarizes and interprets the ancient legal tradition in the great commandment (Mt 22:34-40; Mk 12:28-34; Lk 10:25-28). To the question of a Pharisee, "Teacher, which commandment in the law is the greatest?" Jesus replies:

> "You shall love the Lord your God with all your heart, and with all your soul, and with all your mind." This is the greatest and first commandment. And a second is like it: "You shall love your neighbor as yourself." On these two commandments hang all the law and the prophets. [Mt 22:37-40]

The second commandment requires us to determine the meaning of the terms *neighbor* and *love*. Is neighbor the person who lives next door or in the same village, or the poor and oppressed, or everybody? Luke answers the question by following the commandment with the parable of the Good Samaritan. A neighbor is someone we encounter who is helpless, who needs our mercy, and love is showing mercy to the helpless one. Of the three persons who encounter the helpless man—a priest, a levite, and the Samaritan—only the Samaritan stops and helps. Christ asks: "Which of these three, do you think, was a neighbor to the man who fell into the hands of the robbers?" The questioner answers correctly: "The one who showed him mercy" (Lk 10:36-37). The parable contains the traditional elements of the poor, of mercy and justice, and of the caring person.

Care of the poor and oppressed was a central feature of Jesus' ministry, alongside proclamation of the good news. In Matthew's account of the commissioning of the twelve, Jesus tells them: "As you go, proclaim the good news, 'The kingdom of heaven has come near.' Cure the sick, raise the dead, cleanse the lepers, cast out demons" (Mt 10:7-8). Charity, in the form of miracles of mercy, is a sacred activity that reveals the kingdom of heaven. Christ sends this message to John the Baptist: "the blind receive their sight, the lame walk, the lepers are cleansed, the deaf hear, the dead are raised, and the poor have good news brought to them" (Mt 11:5, cf. Lk 7:22). Those who are healed, "the lame, the maimed, the blind, the mute," respond by giving glory to "the God of Israel" (Mt 15:30-31). Mercy is linked with worship here and in Christ's preaching at Nazareth, where he quotes from Isaiah 61:1-2 that God "has anointed me to bring good news to the poor" (Lk 4:18).

In the teachings of Christ and the prayers and songs of his followers, we have the new revelation: the hungry hunger for the bread of life, the thirsty thirst for living water, the blind see the light of Christ and the deaf hear the good news, lepers are cleansed so that they can perform rites of praise, the dead are raised as signs of the kingdom. Jesus' most explicit teaching about the poor and oppressed in the New Testament occurs in Matthew's account of the great judgment. The passage helps to explain the nature of Christian service. The blessed will inherit the kingdom if they show mercy:

> For I was hungry and you gave me food, I was thirsty and you gave me something to drink, I was a stranger and you welcomed me, I was naked and you gave me

> clothing, I was sick and you took care of me, I was in
> prison and you visited me. [Mt 25:35-36]

Here the symbolic meaning of the poor achieves a deeper dimension than ever before. The poor are Christ, Christ is the poor. The list implies another mode of the real presence of Christ, alongside his presence in the gathered people of God, in the word proclaimed and preached, and in the bread and wine of the eucharist. Because our encounter with the poor brings us face to face with Christ, Christian ministry is not only service to the poor but also, and mainly, service to God.

What occurs between the followers of Christ and the hungry, the thirsty, the stranger, the naked, the sick, and the prisoner is called in the Greek of the New Testament, *diakonia*, which means ministry or service of several kinds, including running errands, delivering messages, and performing assigned tasks. The immediate context is table-service: "For who is greater, the one who is at table or the one who serves? Is it not the one at the table? But I am among you as one who serves" (Lk 22:27)—the Greek translates literally as "the one attending." Assuming the role of waiter, Jesus reverses convention and waits on his disciples. In a similar reversal, at the Last Supper Jesus washes the feet of his followers (Jn 13:1-11). Washing feet is the humble action of a slave—Jesus uses the word *doulos*—but Jesus expands slavery, the abysmal, abject, and involuntary labor of a owned-inferior for an owner-master, into a sacred act under God similar to his sacrifice on the cross. Waiting on others is a divine action as well as an ethical disposition. Christ leaves this supper and this discourse to offer himself on the cross.

Like the Hebrew word commonly translated "servant," the Greek word *diakonos* offers a variety of meanings and problems of definition. It appears to have descended from the Indo-European roots *dia*, meaning thoroughly, and *ken* (or its suffixed o-form *kono*), meaning active. Another possible etymology combines two Greek words meaning "through the dust," and hence servants may have been originally "dusty ones" in the sense of hurried activity on the road. As a Greek common noun, *diakonos* came to mean a particular kind of servant on a prominent level, especially the messenger, go-between, or personal attendant who delivers the orders and carries out the desires and commands of a superior. Because early Christian deacons were also heavily involved in ministry to the needy, the word eventually, centuries later, acquired the present meaning of an ordained servant of charity. This complex verbal ancestry suggests a definition important for our contemporary understanding of the deacon. A deacon is one appointed and given grace to be thoroughly active and dusty in the service of the church and the care of the poor.

Paul sometimes uses the term *diakonos* to refer to himself and others who speak the message of God: Paul and Apollos are "*diakonoi* through whom you came to believe" (1 Cor 3:5). Paul also uses the term *doulos*, slave or lowest form of servant, to signify a menial way of life, voluntarily chosen, referring to himself as "*doulos* of Christ" (Gal 1:10). Far more prominent is his use of the word in the majestic hymn on the Incarnation:

> Let the same mind be in you that was in Christ Jesus, who, though he was in the form of God, did not regard equality with God something to be exploited, but emptied himself, taking the form of a slave, being born in human likeness. [Phil 2:5-7]

In the midst of many parables and sayings about servants, two passages in the gospels have significant implications for the pastoral and sacramental life of the church. In the first passage John tells of the marriage at Cana, which is the first sign to reveal the glory of Christ (Jn 2:1-11). The account includes wine-bearing servants (*diakonoi*) and a chief steward, or headwaiter. This is the imagery of a feast, and these servants are table waiters whose function is to prepare and serve the wine. Obeying an order from an unexpected source, the mother of Jesus, they become agents and witnesses of the transformation of water into wine, of old life into new life.[3] In the second passage Jesus sends two disciples to prepare the passover (Mt 26:17-19, Mk 14:12-16, Lk 22:7-13). They are a model for all who prepare, and in particular they suggest the deacons and others who prepare the altar and set upon it the bread and wine of the eucharist, our celebration of the paschal lamb.

In the grand sweep of *diakonia* and *diakonoi* that fills the New Testament, actual deacons play a tiny role.[4] Even when deacons are mentioned, they may not exercise a formal, cultic office in the community. As we now know, the three orders did not appear full blown on the Day of Pentecost; formal offices evolved gradually, at different times and at different places, during the period in which the Christian scriptures were written and even afterwards. There is a large gap between the deacons we hear of in Paul's letters to the Philippians and Romans (probably written in the 50s), and the deacons of Acts (after 70 CE) and 1 Timothy (near the end of the first century). When deacons are mentioned, however, usually they are linked with bishops, indicating a direct and personal association.

In the salutation of his letter to the Philippians, Paul greets the *episkopoi kai diakonoi*, who, despite the usual translation "bishops and deacons," may be simply "overseers and agents." In Paul's list of gifts exercised for the good of the community (Rom 12:6-8), several gifts suggest roles associated with deacons from early times; the term *diakonia* (in NRSV translated "ministering," in RSV "serving") seems to refer to delivering the word of God. The issue of women as deacons is raised in Romans 16, where Paul winds up his letter by commending to his readers in Rome "our sister Phoebe, a deacon [*diakonon*] of the church at Cenchreae, so that you may welcome her in the Lord as is fitting for the saints, and help her in whatever she may require from you, for she has been a benefactor of many and of myself as well" (16:1-2). Phoebe may be a church emissary in the informal sense, or she may be a formal deacon. When she travels to Rome with Paul's letter, however, she functions in the diaconal role of a messenger or ambassador acting under the direction of a church leader.[5]

The later writings refer clearly to a specific office, and by the last third of the first century we can speak with assurance of deacons in the church. In Acts 6:1-6 Luke does not use the word *diakonos* for the seven men appointed "to wait on tables," and the passage thus cannot be said to speak of historical deacons. But he does use words of service:

> Now during those days when the disciples were increasing in number, the Hellenists complained against the Hebrews because their widows were neglected in the daily distribution [*diakonia*] of food. And the twelve called together the whole community of the disciples and said, "It is not right that we should neglect the word of God in order to wait on [*diakonein*] tables." [Acts 6:1-2]

The preferred work of the apostles is similarly described as prayer and "serving [*diakonia*] the word" (6:4). Luke's intention appears to be not to record the first ordination of deacons in the infant church but, using a past event in conscious anticipation, to comment on *di-*

akonia and the related ministries of bishops and deacons in his own time.[6]

The passage offers guidance in our time also. It tells us that the community bestows orders for ministry at the direction of its leaders, and that the selection is a simple, brief process in which the community chooses the best of many, those "of good standing, full of the Spirit and of wisdom" (6:3). The community discerns those who have gifts, *charismata*, from God. Prior qualification as a faithful Christian seems to be more important than training for service—which is not even mentioned. The appointment, or ordering, consists of a prayer together with the laying on of hands by those who preside, which represents solidarity among those who perform *diakonia*, or commissioned duties, in the community. Their deployment is diverse; although originally chosen for table-waiting, a public function under the direction of the apostles, Stephen goes on to preaching and martyrdom, while Philip spreads the good news and baptizes. It is important to recognize that the community does not ordain simply to fill an occasional need; in the long run the daily ministerial structure of the community is more important than discrete diaconal "jobs."

In 1 Timothy 3:8-13, a list of qualifications for deacons, reflecting a church that is struggling to organize itself, also offers guidance for our time. First, the passage occurs immediately after a similar list for bishops and thus suggests a close relationship between the two offices. Second, it seems to reinforce the scriptural evidence of Romans 16:1 that women are deacons, for the writer gives two parallel and similar lists of qualifications, one for men deacons and one for "women." Third, the passage offers clues for selection based on public respect, and family life based on elemental decency. Deacons, men and women, must be serious, discreet, temperate, and faithful. Like all Christians, deacons "must hold fast to the mystery of the faith with a clear conscience" (3:9). Furthermore, they should be tested to see if they are "blameless," which may refer to a private assessment of character or even to a public examination before election or ratification. Male deacons should be "married only once" (whether concurrently or consecutively, it does not say) and good managers of their families; presumably a similar standard applies to women. There is no mention of formation or function. Deacons who serve well "gain a good standing for themselves and great boldness in the faith that is in Christ Jesus." This promise does not refer to advancement to the presbyterate or episcopate, because grades of Christian office are not mentioned in Scripture and remain foreign to church life for at least three more centuries.

Although actual deacons of the church are minor figures in the New Testament, the ancient tradition and theology whereby the Christian community orders itself appears to be a major element in God's scheme of creation. In our time the biblical tradition provides a guide to *diakonia* and diaconal ministry in the modern church. We need to keep in mind the scriptural sources. God's deliverance of the Hebrews out of oppression and slavery in Egypt moves them to render mercy and justice and to offer true worship. God's deliverance of all people from sin and death, through the servant of the Lord, Christ on the cross, encourages them to wash each other's feet and to break the bread of life.

ENDNOTES

1. Several recent studies trace the tradition in the Hebrew scriptures: Lawrence R. Hennessey, "*Diakonia* and *Diakonoi*

in the Pre-Nicene Church," in *Diakonia: Studies in Honor of Robert T. Meyer*, ed. Thomas Halton and Joseph P. Williams (Washington, DC: Catholic University of America Press, 1986), pp. 60-86, and John M. Cameron, "The Deacon and the Hebrew Scriptures," *Deacon Digest* 5:4 (Nov. 1988), 22-24, 34-36; 6:1 (Feb. 1989), 22-24, 34-36; 6:2 (May 1989), 22-25, 34-36; and 6:3 (Aug. 1989), 22-24, 35-36. For theological reflection on the biblical tradition, see Paulos Mar Gregorios, *The Meaning and Nature of Diakonia* (Geneva: WCC, 1988).

2. For studies of service and servants in the Christian scriptures, see Hennessey, pp. 65-73; Gregorios, pp. 4-26; James M. Barnett, *The Diaconate: A Full and Equal Order* (New York: Seabury Press, 1981), pp. 16-38; and John E. Booty, *The Servant Church: Diaconal Ministry and the Episcopal Church* (Wilton, Conn.: Morehouse-Barlow, 1982), pp. 13-30. For a challenge to the current interpretation of *diakon-* words as referring to care of the needy, see John N. Collins, *Diakonia: Reinterpreting the Ancient Sources* (New York and Oxford: Oxford University Press, 1990).

3. As noted by a deacon, Maylanne Whittall of Toronto, at the biennial NAAD conference on the diaconate, June 1989, *Diakoneo* 11:4 (Sept. 1989), 1.

4. A survey of the scholarship appears in Barnett, pp. 27-38.

5. See Sr. Teresa, CSA, *Women in the Diaconate*, Distinctive Diaconate Studies 23 (1983-86), 1:4. Teresa notes that a church at Cenchreae, a seaport of Corinth, is dedicated to St. Phoebe the Deacon. Her feast day in the Orthodox Church is Sept. 3.

6. Throughout his gospel and Acts, Luke avoids using *diakonos*, a current title for Hermes and other messenger gods (Collins, p. 213).

2

Deacons in the Early Church

*I*n the first few centuries the church developed two practices that have inspired the revival of the order of deacons in the modern church. First, while continuing the ancient tradition of mercy and justice as an obligation of all the faithful, the church added the practice, in many places, of making deacons responsible for the institutional administration of charity. Second, it began to use deacons as officers closely attached to the bishop, ordained as helpers and co-workers in his service. In the major evolutions of church life in the fourth and later centuries, however, both practices gradually underwent drastic changes, including a decline in the importance of the diaconate; the effects are still felt in the life, ministry, and liturgy of Christian communities. Our contemporary understanding of the diaconate, and of ministry in general, in the modern church thus rests partly on issues and problems raised in the early church.

Charity and love

When modern Christians think of service, in the sense of charity, they often have in mind the church of the first three centuries, especially the first century, when believers "would sell their possessions and goods and distribute the proceeds to all, as any had need" (Acts

2:45). In many ways this ideal picture of life as a common and sacred bond is real. Early Christians practiced social charity as individuals and as a community; they collected funds for the poor, and the deacons administered practical care. In the local church of each city or central town, small, persecuted groups of believers lived close to each other and to the neighboring poor. They collected money for the needy at the eucharist and communal meals, visited the sick and those in prison, and sent offerings to Jerusalem and the other churches.

The writings of the early church fathers strongly emphasize the element of *agape* in Christian life. One of the earliest non-canonical documents of the young church is the *Didache*, or *Teaching of the Twelve Apostles*, a Syrian text from early in the second century (c. 110). It begins with a statement about two ways, life and death. The way of life is the way of the great commandment: love God and love your neighbor. The way of life is closely associated with forgiveness, kindness, abstinence, and generosity. It is the way of love. Clement of Rome says in his *Letter to the Corinthians*, about the year 95: "In love the Master took hold of us. For the sake of the love he had for us, Jesus Christ our Lord, by the will of God, gave his blood for us, his flesh for our flesh, and his life for our lives" (49.6).[1]

The principal purpose of *agape*, as early Christians understood it, is to help the poor and others in need. This duty fell equally on all believers. In the middle of the second century Justin Martyr in his *First Apology* writes that the Christians in Rome share their wealth and property with needy persons. After the eucharist, Justin says, the president distributes the collection to orphans and widows, the sick, prisoners, sojourners, and all in need. Tertullian in his *Apology* about the year 197 reports that Christians collect modest amounts of money and expend it for the burial of the poor, for boys and girls without parents and destitute, for the aged quietly confined to their homes, for the shipwrecked; and if there are any in the mines or in the islands or in the prisons, if it be for the reason that they are worshipers of God, then they become the foster sons of their confession. But it is mainly the practice of such a love which leads some to put a brand upon us. "See," they say, "how they love one another," for they themselves hate each other. "And how ready they are to die for one another," they themselves being more inclined to kill each other.

In the early church the *Didache*'s "way of life" was expressed also through a communal meal called an *agape*, or love feast. Practically speaking, the meal was a means of collecting money and food for social relief. Presided over by the bishop, or if he were absent, by a presbyter or deacon, the meal included pi vers, readings, hymn singing, and the giving of pieces of blessed bread (not from the eucharist). The *agape* meal incorporated elements of friendship and community, much like a parish covered-dish supper in the modern church, but its main purpose was charity. Under the supervision of a presbyter or deacon, offerings and leftover food were distributed to the sick, widows, and poor.

Christians also continued the Jewish tradition of individual almsgiving and other relief; the rich and privileged were expected to care for the poor and deprived. But social care was too essential a duty to leave to spontaneous charity or random philanthropy. The church had a strong perception of its corporate responsibility for care, and in each local church the chief agents for charity were deacons acting in the service of the bishop.

After the peace of Constantine in 313, however, the church gradually shifted from a small and familiar organism to a large and often remote institution. Although Christians in many places continued to practice *diakonia* and *agape*, the church's picture of itself as a servant people became hazy. As an imperial institution, with a bureaucracy, terminology, and practices modeled on those of Rome, it absorbed itself in broad issues of doctrine and structure. Eventually, by the middle ages, the official exercise of charity became the obligation chiefly of parish priests and monastic communities. The role of deacons in the church eventually changed to reflect this shift in emphasis.[2]

Ordained to the bishop's service

In the thirty years between Paul of Tarsus and Clement of Rome, the diaconate became established firmly in the young churches; in the second through the fourth centuries, it acquired functions and symbols that have endured to the twentieth. Deacons began to acquire theological significance as *diakonoi* were interpreted as the principal symbols of Jesus in the church.

Three writers near the end of the first century mention deacons. The *Didache* instructs each local church: "Elect for yourselves, therefore, bishops and deacons worthy of the Lord, humble and not lovers of money, truthful and proven; for they also serve you in the ministry of the prophets and teachers" (15:1). The deacons' assistance to their bishops presumably includes service at the eucharistic table. Clement of Rome introduces the typology, later widely copied, of the bishop and presbyter as the Hebrew priest, while the deacon is the Christian equivalent of the Hebrew levite—a ritual waiter in a divinely ordered cult. *The Shepherd of Hermas*, dated early in the second century, depicts the church as a tower under construction in which the square, white fitting-stones are apostles, bishops, teachers, and deacons. Centuries later this metaphor reappears in some icons of deacons, who hold a church building in the left hand (and usually a censer in the right hand). *The*

Shepherd of Hermas also rebukes deacons who plunder widows and orphans and otherwise profit from charity. These early documents tell us that deacons were elected as important officers in the church, acting in a community structure that included oversight of relief for the poor and needy.

Ignatius of Antioch, on his journey to his martyrdom in Rome, wrote letters to seven churches. These letters mention deacons frequently; they are his "fellow servants," integral and respected officers in the church and personal assistants to the bishop. Ignatius is the first Christian to propose a symbolic structure for the three orders: "In like manner let everyone respect the deacons as they would respect Jesus Christ, and just as they respect the bishop as a type of the Father, and the presbyters as the council of God and college of apostles." As sacred symbols, derived from the relationship of Jesus with his Father, deacons are intimately connected with their bishop. They exercise important functions in liturgy and charity. In their active role within the sacred ministry of bishop, presbyters, and deacons, they are "dispensers of the mysteries of Jesus Christ" (a variant of the "mystery of the faith" in 1 Timothy). Yet they are "not deacons of food and drink but officers of the church of God."[3]

Still another writer of the second century who comments on deacons is Justin Martyr, whose *First Apology* gives us the first clear description of the liturgical duties of a deacon:

> After the president has given thanks and all the people have shouted their assent, those whom we call deacons give to each one present to partake of the eucharistic bread and wine and water; and to those who are absent they carry away a portion.

Justin doesn't mention other liturgical functions. Apparently at this time the gospel was sung by a reader, but we do not know who led the intercessions. It is worth noting that deacons administered *both* the bread and the wine (according to ancient custom, mixed with water for sobriety). In a letter supposedly written by Clement of Rome, deacons are to be "as eyes to the bishop" by finding out who is about to sin. Deacons are also to keep order in Christian meetings and inform "the multitude" about the sick, so that they may visit them and supply their needs under the bishop's direction.

We can tell a great deal about the meaning and functions of deacons in the early church from the *Apostolic Tradition* of Hippolytus about the year 215. This work, of immense influence in modern revisions of liturgy, not only reveals the prevailing customs in Rome at the start of the third century, but gives an indication of church order throughout the whole ancient church over an extended period of time. Like a bishop or presbyter, a deacon is elected by all the people of the local church and ordained on the Lord's Day. At the ordination all give assent, and the bishop lays hands on the person chosen, in silence, while all pray for the descent of the Spirit. Hippolytus comments:

> In ordaining a deacon, the bishop alone lays hands, because [a deacon] is ordained not to the priesthood but to the servanthood of the bishop, to carry out commands. [A deacon] does not take part in the council of the clergy, but attends to duties and makes known to the bishop what is necessary . . . .

After the silence, the bishop prays:

> God, who created all things and set them in order by the Word, Father of our Lord Jesus Christ, whom you sent to serve your will and to show us your desires, give

the Holy Spirit of grace and care and diligence to this your servant, whom you have chosen to serve your church and to offer [to bring forward] in your holy of holies the gifts which are offered you by your appointed high priests, so that serving without blame and with a pure heart, he may be counted worthy of this high office and glorify you through your Servant Jesus Christ.[4]

These accounts of ordination rites in Hippolytus have several implications for the modern church.

First, selection. God chooses, as the ordination prayer says, but the choice is wielded by the people of God. The *laos* elect a deacon. We do not know exactly how the process of selection took place, but apparently it involved a gathering of all the Christian people in a city, the local church, who in some way chose one of their number. The bishop's role in the process was to ordain on the next convenient Sunday—implying that he could also refuse. Selection was thus swift and concentrated in the local assembly of Christians, whereas in most churches today the selection process is lengthy and spread among several committees.

Terminology. "Priesthood" and "clergy" used to be synonymous terms. They included the bishop (the high priest) and his presbyters, but not his deacons. Although deacons did not belong to the clergy, they were also not members of a separate group called laity. At that time *laos* still meant all the people of God. The distinction between clergy (*kleros*) and laity (*laos*) was only beginning to be worked out. (By the end of the third century, deacons were considered members of a distinct body called clergy.) Like all Christians, deacons were members of the *laos*, ordained to service but not to the priestly leadership called *kleros*. This early practice stands in contrast to the later, and still current, treatment of clergy and laity as two separate bodies within the one church.

Relationships. Ordination rites symbolize ministerial relationships on several different primary levels. In ancient Rome, the *laos* elected bishops, presbyters, and deacons; hence all three orders had a fundamental relationship with the laity, from whose ranks the ordinand came. This ancient practice has important implications today for connections among church leaders. Within the orders of both bishops and presbyters there is strong collegiality as the "priesthood" [of the bishop]. The ministerial relationship of deacons is primarily with the bishop and not with each other or with the presbyters. The role of deacons as members of the bishop's household or staff, however, provides them with collegial harmony as the "servanthood of the bishop."

Theology. The opening phrases of the ordination prayer in Hippolytus set forth a theology of the diaconate based on Christ as eternal Word and incarnate Servant. God "created all things and set them in order by the Word," and God the Father sent Christ "to serve your will and to show us your desires." Word and Servant are thus scriptural types of the church and the deacon. God's ordering of creation is a type of God's ordering of the church, and the service of Christ (who reveals God and carries out the work of ordered creation) is a type of the service of the deacon. Deacon is to bishop as Word is to God, servant Christ to Father. Like Ignatius of Antioch, therefore, Hippolytus provides a basis for the symbolic appreciation of deacons today.

Functions. The ordination prayer also reveals two areas of function. First, the deacon ordained to the servanthood (or service or ministry) of the bishop is "to serve" the church. The term probably refers not primarily to care of the poor and needy but rather to ecclesial roles such as speaking for, acting for, and attending on the bishop in several important areas, which include social care. Second, the deacon is "to offer"—or, preferably, to bring forward—in the eucharist the gifts offered by the high priest (bishop). These are two different but related liturgical offerings. The deacon presents the people's offerings of bread and wine mixed with water to the bishop, and the bishop offers them to God in the eucharistic prayer. Thus we have the ancient foundation for an ordained ministry that must function both in the world and in the church, as focused in the actions and ministerial relationships of the liturgy.

Another third-century document, the *Didascalia Apostolorum* (Teaching of the Apostles), paints a rich picture of the evolving office of deacon, both man and woman.[5] Here the deacon's work for the bishop clearly includes social welfare: visiting all in need and informing the bishop about those in distress, accepting alms for the bishop, helping the bishop supervise the order of widows. In this work of *diakonia* the deacon works closely with the bishop, "a single soul dwelling in two bodies," often as a full-time, paid factotum, and this activity carries over into the liturgy. One deacon stands by the oblations, and another guards the door as the people enter. The deacon inside sees that each person goes to the proper place (in a congregation segregated by ecclesiastical status, sex, and age) and prevents whispering, sleeping, laughter, and signaling. The deacon makes announcements and at the kiss of peace calls out, "Is there anyone who holds a grudge against his companion?" In the liturgy of baptism the bishop is the normal baptizer, but on occasion he will command the presbyters or deacons to baptize.

The deacon described in early church orders and by Hippolytus and many others comes alive in the person of Laurence of Rome. The church at Rome limited its deacons to seven and each administered a diaconal district.

As the chief or arch deacon of Rome, with especially close and personal ties to his bishop, Laurence had the custody of alms for the poor. On 7 August 258, the bishop Sixtus II and his seven deacons were arrested in the Roman catacombs. As Sixtus and the other six deacons were being carried away for beheading, Laurence cried after him, "Regarding him to whom you entrusted the consecration of the Savior's blood, to whom you have granted fellowship in partaking of the sacraments, would you refuse him a sharing in your death?"[6] Laurence was kept alive because he knew where the silver and gold were. Finally he gathered the poor, the lame, and the blind for whom he had cared, showed them to the city prefect, and said, "These are the treasures of the church." He was martyred on August 10, supposedly roasted alive on a gridiron but probably beheaded like his bishop.

Another early deacon with close ties to his bishop was Vincent of Saragossa, martyred on 22 January 304. Vincent was not only the eyes and ears of his bishop, but literally his mouth. Because Valerius stuttered badly, Vincent often preached for him. According to legend, they were arrested by the governor of Spain, threatened with torture and death, and pressured to renounce their faith. Vincent said, "Father, if you order me, I will speak." Valerius replied, "Son, as I have committed you to dispense the word of God, so I now charge you to answer in vindication of the faith which we defend." Vincent defied the governor and was tortured to death.

As with the men, the legends of women deacon saints of the early church tell us more than any other document. In addition to Phoebe, these saints include a prominent martyr, the aged Apollonia, burned to death by a mob in Alexandria on 2 February 249. Refusing to renounce the faith, she walked into a bonfire her tormentors had set. Because they first knocked out her teeth, she became the patron of dentists and toothache victims. According to an apocryphal legend in the early church, the female martyr Thekla was converted in the 50s or 60s at Iconium, became a deacon (perhaps), and after much persecution for her dedication to virginity, was martyred at the age of ninety. Thekla was immensely popular in the early church. The Orthodox honor her as the first woman martyr, parallel to Stephen, with a feast day on September 23.

Scholars may question the historical accuracy of these legends about Laurence and Vincent, Apollonia and Thekla, and other early martyrs, but they tell us a good deal about deacons in the early church. They stood close to their bishop, they brought help to the poor and brought the word to the people, and they held the mystery of the faith with a clear conscience, even to death.

The end of the third century and beginning of the fourth was a time of great change for the church and its deacons. After Constantine and his co-emperor adopted a policy of toleration for the Christian church in 313, and thus it began to grow, new rules evolved to define the roles of deacons. Some of these governed the moral and sexual conduct of presbyters and deacons. In about 250 Cyprian and other bishops had written with approval of the excommunication of a deacon "who dallied often with a virgin," while later on there may also have been concern about nepotism. At the end of the third century, the reform-minded Council of Elvira tried to impose celibacy with the rule, widely ignored, that bishops, presbyters, and deacons "are to keep themselves away from their wives and are not to beget children," while the Council of Ancyra in 314 set the rule that deacons may marry after ordination only if they announce their intention to marry before ordination; otherwise they are to be deposed.

Rules governing clerical conduct were repeated and reinforced by the Council of Nicaea in 325. No cleric may have a woman living with him, except his mother, sister, aunt, or other woman beyond suspicion (Canon 4). Because of "great disorder and contentions," no cleric is allowed "to move from city to city" (Canon 15). But one canon is more ominous than all the rest: deacons must keep within their rank, not sit with the presbyters, and not give communion to presbyters, for they are "the servants of the bishop and . . . less than presbyters" (Canon 18). By the end of the fourth century, a male deacon is defined in negative terms. He may not bless, baptize, or offer the eucharist, but he may excommunicate those of lesser rank. A subdeacon, lector, cantor, and deaconess may do even less, "for they are the inferior of deacons."[7] The church of this period seemed more interested in hierarchical rank than in service of the bishop defined as ministry carrying out the work of God.

The most celebrated eastern deacon of this period was Ephrem of Edessa, whom the Syrians called "the harp of the Holy Spirit." He may have accompanied his bishop, James of Nisibis, to the Council of Nicaea. After the fall of Nisibis to the Persians in 363, he retired to a cave near Edessa, where he lived a harsh life, preached in the city, cared for the poor and sick, and wrote hymns, sung by a choir of women, as a weapon against the gnostic and Arian heresies. In combating heresy, Ephrem considered himself an agent of his bishop. His writings in Syriac are famous both for their scriptural inspiration and for their metaphorical style. Still another Syrian poet was the deacon Romanos the Melodist, who in the sixth century moved to Constantinople, where he wrote metrical sermons and hymns. Some of his *kontakia*, brief hymns in the form of prayer, are still sung in eastern churches.

Several women deacons are remembered partly because of famous relatives or friends, such as Nonna, mother of the bishop Gregory Nazianzus. In another prominent family of the fourth century, the bishops Gregory of Nyssa and Basil the Great had as their elder sister the deacon Macrina the Younger, famous in her own right as head of a community of nuns on the family estate in Cappadocia; her friend the deacon Lampadia led a chorus of virgins. In Constantinople the deacon Olympias, a rich widow, ran a convent called the Olympiados that included four deacons and some two hundred fifty virgins. She taught catechumens and cared for widows, the old, the sick, and the poor. When John Chrysostom, the new bishop, arrived in 397, she became his friend, advisor, and benefactor, and upon his exile she suffered persecution from his enemies.

The most famous woman deacon of the West is Radegund of Poitiers, who died in 587. As a child she was kidnapped from Thuringia and eventually forced to marry the brutish king Clothaire I of the Franks. She endured him for ten years until he murdered her brother. Radegund then fled to Noyon, where she persuaded the bishop to ordain her a deacon, and began a ministry of caring for the sick, including lepers, and visiting prisoners. After her ordination she founded Holy Cross monastery near Poitiers, which at her death numbered some two hundred nuns.

The lessons of the early diaconate

The development of the diaconate in the first three centuries and the changes of subsequent centuries are not isolated incidents in the history of the early church. They have meaning today, shedding light on issues in the modern church and providing guidance for our understanding.

One of these is the question of women deacons. Some branches of the church, including some provinces of the Anglican communion, do not yet ordain women as deacons. Even in places where women deacons are accepted, they are sometimes treated as inferior to men deacons. The historical evidence, however, supports the ordination of women as deacons in the early church. They functioned in ways that were parallel to the role of men deacons, caring for women and children as the men cared for men, although they often had subordinate status. Numerous and widespread in the East, especially in Syria and Greece, women deacons flourished in the fourth through the seventh centuries and continued to function in Constantinople until the twelfth century. Although less numerous in the West, and entirely absent in Rome, they were ordained in Gaul and other areas where women exercised authority. Their ordination rites paralleled those of the men, and they received the *orarion*, or stole. Frequently these women were the wives of men deacons or presbyters, until mandatory celibacy abolished clerical families. Some were the wives of bishops: when the man was made a bishop and separated from his wife, the woman, if suited for the office, became a deacon.

In the East, men and women deacons functioned both pastorally and liturgically. In the eucharist women deacons ministered together in church, oversaw and made announcements to the women, who were seated off to one side, or in the gallery, led their responses, supervised their offerings, and administered their communion. They arranged the lamps, washed the vessels, and mixed the water and wine in the chalice. In liturgies composed only of women, they read the lessons and taught. In baptism, in which the candidates were nude, they anointed and clothed the female neophytes. They took communion to the housebound and chaperoned interviews between male clerics and women. The *Didascalia*, expanding on Ignatius of Antioch, says that the woman deacon stands "in the position of the Holy Spirit."

In the West, after about the fourth century, the position of women deacons appears to have suffered as a result of the high regard in which virgins were held, a regard not extended to widows. When women deacons reached Gaul, typically it was widows who became deacons. Most likely their duties were similar to those in the East, with an emphasis on teaching. The document of Nicaea has something to tell us about the status of women deacons. In mentioning the problem of the Paulianists, anti-Trinitarian heretics who are returning to the church, canon 19 of Nicaea states that they are to be rebaptized, and their clergy reordained or deposed. "However, we note concerning those who have assumed the garb of deaconess: because they have not had any ordination, they are to be numbered among the laity."[8] The feminine form *diakonissa* appears here for the first time in a legal document. By referring to the garbed but unordained heretics as lay persons, the canon implies that ordained women deacons (who also wear special dress) are members of the clergy.

After the fourth century, presbyters became parish priests and bishops the administrators of dioceses. With this change, only a few highly placed deacons could be the eyes and ears of the bishop, and most deacons became instead clerics in transit to the priesthood. Before, deacons were the agents of the bishop's oversight of *diakonia* in the parish; now they tended to be actors playing a liturgical bit part. This shift resulted in a new distinction between diocesan and parish deacons, one which has reappeared in our time. Before the fourth century, deacons in a church or parish had been a small group attached to the bishop, like Laurence of Rome, who is a classic example of the early diaconate. After the peace of Constantine, however, deacons were scattered over the diocese and became pastoral assistants to presbyters. Eventually they were detached from their bishop, seen as inferior to presbyters, and functioned mainly in the liturgy—servants not so much of *diakonia* in the fullest sense as of sacred rites alone, on the threshold of the priesthood.

We have a similar situation in the modern church. Bishops are chief pastors of dioceses, not pastors of parishes, so when we require our deacons to serve directly under the bishop, this means something vastly different from what it meant to Laurence or Vincent. Parish pastors in most denominations function much as early bishops did—except that they may not ordain. The question for the modern church is twofold: first, how is the deacon to serve adequately under both the bishop and the priest, and second, how is the bishop to get back in the business of overseeing *diakonia*?

Another issue facing the contemporary church is the balance of roles in the liturgy according to order and appropriate function. In the second century the scriptural definition of *diakonos* as chief table waiter was fully acted out in the eucharist—they set the table and served the bread and wine. In the third century, deacons invited the people to exchange the kiss of peace, received the offerings of bread and wine, and brought them to the bishop, but they served only the wine. By the fourth century, diaconal functions expanded into the liturgy of the word. Deacons began to represent angels and messengers as well as table waiters. They proclaimed the gospel (formerly read by a reader), sang the litany of intercession, announced stages of the liturgy, and at the paschal vigil blessed the candle.

Gradually, however, priests took over the diaconal functions. This resulted in a loss to both orders, and hence in a loss of symbolism for the church. As the priesthood reached to include within itself all ministry, it lost priestly presence. The main priestly function, singing the eucharistic prayer, became reduced to a mostly inaudible mumble in an action barely visible to the congregation. As the diaconate became absorbed into the priesthood, as a step on the hierarchical pyramid, it lost presence, the special significance of those who are publicly visible as servants and who spend their lives in active service. Their roles in the church became unbalanced.

In modern liturgies throughout the West, the church has recovered almost everything deacons slowly accumulated over four centuries. The problem facing the church now is how to keep a balance among the diversity of roles. Deacons may share some of their role with other members of the *laos*; the Episcopal Church does not restrict the prayers of the people or the administration of the wine to deacons. Some other Anglican churches, following the practice in first three centuries, will even allow any baptized person to proclaim the gospel. Bishops and presbyters may also relinquish to others their servant functions in the liturgy, but the other members of the *laos* also need to show restraint and respect for the development of liturgical tradition in the early church. Liturgy should accurately symbolize both the priesthood and the *diakonia* carried out on the cross and in the world.

The issue of diversity of roles, however, includes far more than orderly worship. Liturgy reflects the entire life of the church, and the balance of roles in the liturgical assembly reveals all too accurately how the bishop, presbyters, deacons, and all the faithful of a diocese relate to each other, minister as priests and servants in the world, and serve the will of God.

ENDNOTES

1. Unless otherwise noted, patristic texts in this chapter are from William A. Jurgens, ed., *The Faith of the Early Fathers*, 3 vols. (Collegeville, Minn.: Liturgical Press, 1970-79).

2. Barnett, *Diaconate*, pp. 43-131; Hennessey, "Diakonia and *Diakonoi* in the Pre-Nicene Church," pp. 74-86; Sr. Teresa, CSA, *Women in the Diaconate*; J. Robert Wright, "The Emergence of the Diaconate," *Liturgy: Diakonia* 2:4 (Fall 1982), 17-23, 67-71; and Edward P. Echlin, *The Deacon in the Church: Past and Future* (Staten Island, N.Y.: Alba House, 1971), pp. 14-94.

3. *Phil* 4.1; *Trall* 3.1 (see also *Magn* 6.1, *Smyrn* 12.2); *Trall* 2.3.

4. From the Latin in H. B. Porter, Jr., *The Ordination Prayers of the Ancient Western Churches*, Alcuin Club Collections 49 (London: SPCK, 1967), p. 10.

5. See Sebastian Brock and Michael Vasey, ed., *The Liturgical Portions of the Didascalia*, Grove Liturgical Studies 29 (Bramcote, Notts.: Grove Books, 1982), pp. 11-12, 15-16, 22-23. See also Robert Nowell, *The Ministry of Service: Deacons in the Contemporary Church* (New York: Herder and Herder, 1968), pp. 24-29.

6. Ambrose, *De Off* I.41.214. The reference to "consecration" means at least administration of the wine—but perhaps more.

7. From AC 8.17-20 in Franz Xaver von Funk, ed., *Didascalia et Constitutiones apostolorum*, 2 vols. (Paderborn: Schoeningh, 1905), 1:522-525. For a recent English translation, see W. Jardine Grisbrooke, ed., *The Liturgical Portions of the Apostolic Constitutions: A Text for Students*, Alcuin/GROW Liturgical Studies 13-14 (Bramcote, Notts.: Grove Books, 1990), pp. 75-76.

8. Translation of Canon 19 by Teresa, *Women in the Diaconate*, 2:34.

3

Episcopal Church: Early Deacons

*U*ntil recent years, the deacon most church-goers saw and knew was a young man in an interim state. After graduating from seminary, he awaited his ordination to the priesthood, passed a brief internship, and learned his craft from an older, wiser priest. This temporary office inherited from the classic diaconate only the name and liturgy of deacon. By its very nature it was intended neither to provide *diakonia* to the poor and needy, nor to assist the bishop in important matters, but to season apprentice clerics in sacerdotal and—particularly after the Reformation—pastoral ministry. This view of the diaconate was common to the Anglican, Roman Catholic, Orthodox, and some protestant churches. But early in the nineteenth century renewal movements, evangelical and catholic revivals, the rediscovery of patristic sources, new attitudes toward the poor, and new opportunities in mission fields slowly caused the churches to respond with experiments in diaconal ministry.

Since the early nineteenth century, the Episcopal Church in particular has seen four types, or "waves," of deacons. There are missionary or indigenous deacons (male), deaconesses (female), perpetual deacons (male), and deacons today (male and female).[1] These are not neatly exclusive categories; to a large extent they overlap. But they illustrate how the order of deacons has developed and changed as the response of the church to the needs of the world in different historical circumstances. In this chapter I will speak of the first three waves, the early deacons who preceded the deacons of today.

Missionary or indigenous deacons

The missionary or indigenous deacon, existing from the 1840s through the 1930s and usually ordained on an ad hoc basis, was virtually unknown to most Episcopalians in settled parts of the nation, and was rare even on the frontier. It was a diverse and often eccentric ministry, as the following stories will reveal. One of the first deacons in the Episcopal Church of whom we have extensive knowledge worked in what is now the diocese of Western North Carolina. In 1842 Bishop Levi S. Ives of North Carolina decided to begin mission work in a wild area near Boone where two valleys cross. He bought two thousand acres and called the area Valle Crucis. There he established a monastic community called the Society of the Holy Cross and for the first monk professed a farmer, William West Skiles.

Skiles was born in North Dakota and came to Valle Crucis in 1844 at the age of thirty-seven. He supervised the farming operation and dairy herd, taught school, kept store, practiced medicine, raised funds to build the local Church of St. John the Baptist (contributing a third of the $700 construction cost), and became the spiritual leader of the community. Ives ordained Skiles a deacon in August 1847. In 1852 Ives resigned his office, sold the land, and became a Roman Catholic. The monastic order and school disbanded, but Skiles was the only one of the original monks not to marry. "Brother Skiles," as he was called, continued to care for the poor valley people until he died on 8 December

1862, and his body was buried next to the church he helped to build.[2]

Skiles was a missionary deacon, ordained to provide for religious life on the frontier. As the American people pushed west, beyond the settled life of the eastern seaboard, the need grew for trained missionaries who were part of frontier society. There were probably priests and deacons ordained casually to fill the need in remote communities. Rather late, in 1871, by a resolution of General Convention, the church eventually made canonical provision for deacons. From 1871 through 1904, under this canon, men were ordained deacon for missionary fields and ethnic—especially Native American—communities to which they were indigenous.

Two outstanding examples of missionary or indigenous deacons ordained in the late nineteenth century are Milnor Jones and David Pendleton Oakerhater. In 1895 Bishop Joseph Blount Cheshire of North Carolina decided to revive the Valle Crucis mission around another fascinating character. This was Milnor Jones, born in 1848 of a prominent Maryland family, who fought as a Confederate soldier and then became a lawyer in Texas before suffering injury in a riding accident. Left with a limp, he devoted the rest of his life to God. After graduating from seminary at Sewanee and being ordained deacon in 1876, he decided to remain a deacon and, in the words of his bishop, to make himself "all things to the lowly whom he had chosen for his own." Most of his work was among the poor people of Western North Carolina, in 1879-92 around Tryon and in 1894-96 at Valle Crucis. He died in Baltimore in 1916.

We know about Jones from his biographer, Bishop Cheshire. *Milnor Jones, Deacon and Missionary* (actually a long obituary, dated 1916) was published in the diocesan newspaper and later as a pamphlet. Jones was outspoken, crusty, and cantankerous, qualities that delighted the bishop. He was especially fond of denouncing the local Baptists and Methodists, and sometimes came close to inciting a riot. One mob even threatened the bishop. Nevertheless, Bishop Cheshire took delight in a deacon "who did not scruple on occasion to tell his bishop that the sermon he [the bishop] had just preached, 'did no more good than pouring water on a duck's back.'" An undisciplined oddball who cared nothing for settled work, and who preferred to minister in backwoods places, Jones traveled the mountain trails in the saddle, made friends of all he met, handed out prayer books, baptized everyone he could (often by immersion in a nearby creek), preached wild sermons from house to house, and only on rare occasion encountered his bishop, a priest, or any other member of the Episcopal establishment.

Another early deacon was David Pendleton Oakerhater of Oklahoma, whose Cheyenne name means "Sundancer" or "Making Medicine." Oakerhater was a war chief; as a young man, he distinguished himself for bravery as a member of an elite Cheyenne warrior society. After the futile battle of Adobe Walls in 1874, in which warriors of five tribes attacked a camp of white buffalo hunters in Texas, he was captured as one of the ring leaders and taken in chains, without trial, to the cavalry post at Fort Sill, Oklahoma. Later he was moved to Fort Marion, an old military prison at St. Augustine, Florida. At prison Oakerhater showed his natural leadership. Mainly through his friendship with the young daughter of Senator George Hunt Pendleton of Ohio, he converted to Christ, was sent to upstate New York to receive a Christian education, and was baptized on 6 October 1878.

Ordained deacon on 7 June 1881, Oakerhater left immediately for the Cheyenne nation of Oklahoma accom-

panied by a white priest, John B. Wicks. He returned to
the people he had once led in war. When he met their
leaders for the first time as a Christian he spoke in
words long remembered among the Cheyenne. His
address began:

> Men, you all know me. You remember when I led you
> out to war I went first and what I told you was true.
> Now I have been away to the east and I have learned
> about another captain, the Lord Jesus Christ, and he is
> my leader. He goes first, and all he tells me is true. I
> come back to my people to tell you to go with me now in
> this new road, a war that makes all for peace, and
> where we [ever] have only victory.[3]

In the Indian territory of northwest Oklahoma, Oakerhater touched the lives of hundreds of Cheyenne
through his counseling, preaching, baptizing, and teaching. Within three years the whole nation converted to
Christ. Among the new Christians was Whirlwind, a
great peace chief, who at the turn of the century gave
land for the new Episcopal mission at an old Indian village near Watonga. This religious and educational center
for the Cheyenne still bears the name of Whirlwind Mission of the Holy Family. In 1904 Oakerhater opened a
school at the mission that lasted until 1917, when the
church closed it under government pressure.

The priest left after three years because of ill health,
and soon Oakerhater was alone. The leaders of the Episcopal Church abandoned work among the Indians in
Oklahoma. For twelve years Oakerhater was the only ordained Episcopalian in what is now the state of Oklahoma. Even after he retired in 1917 on a small
pension, he continued to counsel and preach, marry the
young and bury the dead, baptize, visit the sick, and
find food for the hungry, until he died in 1931.

Many other American Indians ministered as deacons among their people. By the 1860s, Dakota deacons included Daniel C. Hemans, Philip Johnson Wahpehan (called Philip the Deacon), and Christian Taopi (a former warrior, called Wounded One). The Kiowa deacon Paul Zotom traveled with Oakerhater on his trip west in 1881, but his work soon failed. Thomas P. Ashley ministered among the Sioux around the turn of the century until he was divorced in 1907. A Canadian of mixed Indian and white ancestry, Wellington Jefferson Salt worked with the Chippewa from 1911 until his death in 1920. Athabascan deacons include William Loola of Fort Yukon, Alaska, ordained in 1903, and Albert Tritt, ordained in the 1920s.[4]

These missionary or indigenous deacons of the nineteenth and early twentieth centuries really functioned as priests. Often solitary, exercising their ministries without oversight and rarely in contact with their bishop, these men kept the Christian faith alive among their people. They presided over a community and built it up by preaching, teaching, and caring. These deacons administered the sacraments in every way except the one essential to leading a community in the complete Christian life: they were not permitted to preside at the eucharist.

Deaconesses

The deaconess movement arose out of a sincere desire in many churches to organize women to work with the poor and sick. In the early nineteenth century this desire emerged in the Lutheran churches of Germany and helped shape a definition of *diakonia* that has lasted to this day: care of the needy. In the middle ages, social care was handled mainly by parish priests and monastic orders, but by the sixteenth century this system of charity had begun to break down. In the early nineteenth century, in the rubble of the Napoleonic wars and the human wreckage of the industrial age, secular and Christian social reformers drew attention to the plight of the poor, and both the evangelical revival and the Oxford movement awakened interest in social care as a crucial concern of the church. In Germany in 1831 the Lutheran pastor Theodore Fliedner founded a training institution at Kaiserswerth for women deaconesses after the New Testament model. Their pastors "consecrated" them, although this was not considered ordination. These women began with ministries such as visiting the sick and poor in the parish, teaching young children and girls, and bringing ill children back to their infirmary for nursing. They shaped the Kaiserswerth institution into the deaconess motherhouse (sisterhood or association) movement, exercising a ministry of social welfare that flourishes to this day. In 1849 Fliedner brought four Lutheran deaconesses to Pittsburgh, Pennsylvania, and began a work which continues in the twentieth century. Florence Nightingale trained at Kaiserswerth in 1851 and returned to England to found a secular school for nurses.

Anglicans in England and America soon attempted to imitate Fliedner, and in England a group of women dedicated themselves in 1861 "to minister to the necessities of the church" as "servants of the church." On 18 July 1862 Bishop Archibald Campbell Tait of London (who had visited Kaiserswerth in 1855) admitted Elizabeth Ferard to the office of deaconess with the laying on of hands. Ferard was thus the first woman deacon in the Church of England after a lapse of several centuries. She founded a community of women in 1861 which gradually grew into a religious order of deaconesses still in existence, the (formerly Deaconess) Community of St. Andrew.[5]

In America interest in the German deaconess movement began earlier than in England but did not immediately result in ordained deaconesses. In 1845 William Augustus Muhlenberg, rector of the Church of the Holy Communion in New York City, formed a sisterhood based on the German model. The first formal admission of deaconesses in the Episcopal Church took place forty years later in Alabama. The first bishop of Alabama, Nicholas H. Cobbs, planned a cathedral in Montgomery with a group of institutions around the building and, more importantly, around the bishop as "the heart" of the diocese. These were to include a house for deacons (for missionary and pastoral work) and a house for deaconesses (for care of the sick and poor), but the Civil War interrupted these plans. In late December 1864 his successor, Richard Hooker Wilmer, "instituted"—without laying on hands—three deaconesses, who formed a sisterhood after the Kaiserswerth model, with a constitution and rules approved by the bishop, and set to work caring for the many orphans left by the war. By 1885 Wilmer had overcome his scruples about imposing hands, and he set apart two deaconesses, Mary W. Johnson on Epiphany and Mary Caroline Friggell on St. Peter's Day. Strictly speaking, they were the first ordained deaconesses in the Episcopal Church.[6]

In 1889 General Convention passed Canon 10, "Of Deaconesses," which remained in effect, occasionally amended, until it was repealed in 1970. The existence of the canon was the result of the lobbying efforts, starting in 1871, of William Reed Huntington, rector of Grace Church, New York City. His parish immediately provided facilities for deaconesses and established a training center called Huntington House. Other training schools were opened in San Francisco, New Orleans, Minneapolis, Philadelphia, Berkeley, and Chicago. Most of these, funded by the diocese or local supporters, encountered financial difficulties and soon closed. Some became general training schools. In 1953, with the help of Millard Street, suffragan bishop of Chicago, the Central House for Deaconesses was established, with a house in Evanston, Illinois. This continued in existence until it changed its name in 1974 to the National Center for the Diaconate.

Deaconesses in the Episcopal Church were "unmarried or widowed"—that is, celibate—for most of the existence of the order. A substantial change in the canon occurred in 1964, when General Convention, in response to the spirit of the times, removed the phrase "unmarried or widowed." But the ancient order, as restored in the Episcopal Church, had already begun to decline. Thus the final form of Canon 51, "Of Deaconesses," adopted in 1964, begins:

> A woman of devout character and proved fitness may be ordered Deaconess by any Bishop of this Church, subject to the provisions of this Canon.

The canon goes on to list charitable and pastoral functions. A deaconess is to care for "the sick, the afflicted, and the poor," to instruct in the faith, to prepare candidates for baptism and confirmation, to "work among women and children," and to "organize and carry on social work" (including the education of women and children). They are also to assist at baptism, to read the daily offices and litany "in the absence of the Minister," and when licensed by the bishop "to give instruction or deliver addresses at such services."

Above all else, the order of deaconesses was a service order with a strong sense of community. Although its members often lived apart and in lonely circumstances, they supported each other in prayer, giving, and the common life. It was a society of women church workers, an historic order of deaconesses, and a quasi-religious order—a community of sisters with distinctive dress and pectoral cross, austere lifestyle, and concept of social work. Although the dress appeared to many to be a religious habit, it was modeled on Kaiserswerth apparel or the normal dress of the early nineteenth century, with a simple veil and collar. In England celibacy was not required except in the Community of St. Andrew; there was a married deaconess as early as the 1880s. Deaconesses worked in many different settings: as parish assistants, teachers, institutional and school administrators, prison and hospital chaplains, inner-city workers, and missionaries, often in remote areas such as Appalachia and Nevada. A few were wealthy, but most lived in poverty and performed hard work for low wages over many years of loyal dedication.

One important source for the work of deaconesses are the dozen diaries and hundreds of letters, pictures, and other artifacts of Mary Douglass Burnham (1832-1904), which her great-granddaughter found in a trunk in the attic. Long before she was set apart as deaconess, Burnham helped to found the Dakota League in Massachusetts in 1864, in support of Indian missions, and in the 1870s she went to work among the Ponka tribe in Nebraska. There she taught women and girls to sew. Her letters indicate the practical nature of Christian charity which deaconesses had to perform. In one letter she writes, "Between women sitting on the floor, some with babies strapped to a board beside them or older ones crawling around, it requires considerable dexterity to get from one side to the other without doing any damage." She also assisted the sick and dying, although she knew "so little about sickness that I don't venture much beyond Nitro for fever and Quinine for chills." Throughout her life she remained keenly interested in Indian work and influenced Oakerhater in his conversion to Christianity. Later she served as head of several charity institutions and hospitals until shortly before her death.[7]

Another deaconess, Julia A. Clark, spent five years in Yunan, China, in the war-torn district of Hankow. Her work included carrying supplies to hospital bases and helping with nursing. She was several times under bomb attack; often she had to prepare bodies for burial. Her story includes one account interesting for its implications about liturgy and authority:

> Perhaps some of you may be shocked when I tell you of another thing that I did. The clergy were hard-pressed. Near the air bases, there would sometimes be over 100 aviators at the Holy Communion. One of the missionary bishops over there asked me to assist, I being a deaconess. I could only ask him to speak to my bishop and to the other bishops. You see, the Church is all one Church in China—English, Chinese, American—all making one Holy Catholic Church. I told the Chinese bishop that I was the American deaconess, and that American deaconesses did not assist at the Holy Communion. And he said, "You are a Chinese deaconess out here." Everyone consented, so I thought it right to do what I was asked to do. I administered the cup. I thought that I would wear just a cotta, but they had me wear a surplice, and they insisted upon a stole. So I wore that also, over the shoulder as a deacon does.[8]

The order of deaconesses also included some feisty characters. One was Mary Sandys Hutton, who worked in the Blue Ridge mountains of Virginia from 1934 on. This remarkable woman was paralyzed from polio and had walked on crutches since the age of three. Nevertheless, she founded missions, directed a doctor's clinic and a clothing bureau, visited mountain homes, preached, conducted prayer book services, held revivals, ran a school bus, and sponsored children for baptism (as a deaconess, she was not allowed to baptize), many of whom were named after her. Several documents testify to the love and respect in which mountain folk held her. At her funeral the preacher recalled one incident. Hutton was conducting morning prayer at a remote mission where the people were not speaking to each other. She decided to delay the service until there was peace.

> "I want everybody here to turn to the person next to him and shake hands," she said. "If you can say, 'I'm glad you're here,' do it. If you can't, don't. You won't fool God and you won't fool me. But you can shake hands."

"They just stared at me and did nothing," she remembered. "I said, 'I'm not going to start services until you do. You can have a Christian church or belong to the devil.' They shook hands."

On another occasion a mountaineer came into her house with a shotgun and announced that he had a message from God to kill her. "That's strange," she said. "I was just talking to God, and he didn't mention it to me. Perhaps we'd better talk to him together." After an hour or so the man departed, leaving his shotgun. The deaconess sent it back to him.[9]

Another spunky deaconess was Harriet M. Bedell (1875-1969), who spent ten years at Whirlwind Mission in Oklahoma and sixteen years with Indians in Alaska before coming to the Mikasuki tribe of the Seminoles. In Florida she lived in a simple four-room house on the Tamiami Trail, in the midst of the Everglades. The Mikasuki gradually came to trust her, and she was the only white person they would speak to. In her old age the diocese wanted her to move into a religious community, but she said, "No. No. This is my place. They need me, and I am not frightened out here. The Indians are always watching me, just as God is watching over me." During more than a quarter-century with the Mikasuki, she converted some of the families, but the Seminoles were not ready to accept Christ as a tribe. In 1960 she quoted one old medicine man, "You just keep on telling us, and by'm by we do what you say."[10]

In Nevada the presence of indefatigable and underpaid deaconesses in many of the rural communities of the 30s and 40s helped to pave the way for acceptance of new forms of women's ministry in the 70s and 80s. At Pyramid Lake, on the Northern Band Paiute Reservation, the older women remember the presence of "the nuns" (deaconesses in habits) who worked as medical missionaries in conjunction with a circuit riding physician, catechized the children and young people, and did a wide variety of other ministries.

One Nevada deaconess, Lydia Ramsay, worked at St. Andrew's, Battle Mountain, in the late 30s. She illustrates the gifts which women can bring to isolated communities in a harsh environment. One of her responsibilities was coordinating a program called Church School by Mail. She would drive the unpaved roads of northern Nevada's vast range land looking for children to enroll. Her preferred tactic was to do her scouting on wash day. Anytime she saw children's clothes on the wash line she would stop and visit, and sign the family up.

One of Nevada's historic deaconesses is still active. Mary Hetler ministered at Christ Church, Pioche, as deaconess in charge, and she served the diocese as a whole through her work in Christian education and at the diocesan camp, Galilee. In the latter capacity she usually picked up and delivered children along her route from Pioche to Lake Tahoe—a trip of roughly 450 miles each way. Later she married Jim Bradshaw and moved to nearby Caliente; as was customary in those days, she was deposed from the diaconate upon her marriage. Her ministry, however, continued. Fifty-three years after her setting apart, and now restored to the diaconate, Mary Bradshaw coordinates senior citizens transportation for all of remote Lincoln County.[11]

Deaconesses worked among the mountaineers of Virginia, the range dwellers of Nevada, the Cheyenne of Oklahoma, the Ponkas of Nebraska, the Eskimos and Athabascans of Alaska, the Seminoles of Florida, the Lakota of South Dakota. They worked as missionaries in Liberia, China, the Philippines, and Brazil. They were directors of religious education in big parishes and social workers in inner-city slums. They lived in mountain huts and primitive fishing camps. They cared for the sick and the poor, helped at childbirth and buried the dead, worked as registered nurses and certified teachers. They taught the Bible and under the most exhausting and crude circumstances witnessed to Jesus Christ as Lord and Savior.

In the eighty-six years of its existence, 1885 through 1970, the order of deaconesses in the Episcopal Church attracted almost five hundred women. In many dioceses it was a vital, important ministry to the poor and sick. In its last years the order faded, no longer popular as a special ministry for women, and fell victim to the changing roles, opportunities, and aspirations of women beginning to seek equality with men in the church and in society. In its last decade only two or three ordinations took place every year, and a few of the remaining deaconesses eventually became priests. The last woman ordained deaconess, on 20 September 1970, was Shirley Woods, who became a priest in 1977 and was dean of the School for Deacons in the diocese of California until she retired in 1990.

Perpetual deacons

After World War II the Episcopal Church grew rapidly in membership. To satisfy the need for sacramental and pastoral assistance in parishes, General Convention in 1952 restored the diaconate for men, commonly called "perpetual deacons." The 1952 canon describes this deacon as

> a man of devout character and proved fitness, desirous to serve in the capacity of Deacon without relinquishing his secular occupation and with no intention of seeking advancement to the Priesthood . . . [I.34.10(a)]

He must be at least thirty-two years old. Candidacy lasts at least six months. He is examined in a list of subjects, but educational requirements are lower than those for the priesthood. The deacon "shall exercise his Ministry as assistant in any parish or parishes to which, at the request or with the consent of the Rector and Vestry, he may be assigned by the Ecclesiastical Authority," but may not be in charge of a congregation. A final clause provides for a deacon "who may afterward desire to be advanced to the Priesthood." An amendment in 1964 allowed the deacon to be in charge of a congregation under certain circumstances. In 1967 an amendment provided modifications of the educational requirements for an indigenous deacon.

The provision for perpetual deacons was moderately popular. From 1952 through 1970, when canonical changes introduced women deacons and altered the nature of the order, 517 men were ordained under the canon. Most were ordained in a few dioceses such as Michigan and California (where Bishop James A. Pike preferred to ordain groups of deacons just before Christmas each year). Most were older men, raised out of the congregations in which they were to function as deacon, often personally picked by the parish priest, and locally trained. At the end of 1990 there were 148 perpetual deacons still alive and in the diaconate. Actually, these numbers are misleading, because male deacons of the perpetual type—curates, or sacramental and pastoral assistants—continued to be ordained after 1970, but with decreasing frequency, and after 1980 it was a rare bishop who ordained an old-style deacon for ministry solely within the parish.

At their best, perpetual deacons stayed close to the people and found their ministry in visiting the sick and needy of the parish and bringing them the sacrament. Rectors came and went, but the deacon remained, a perpetual curate. A good example of this is found in a novel entitled *The Deacon*, written by a perpetual deacon, Robert E. Gard of Wisconsin.[12] In the story a deacon narrates a tale about the ghost of Bishop Jackson Kemper, the famous missionary in that part of the country, who benevolently haunts Grace Church in Madison (a parish famous in the liturgical movement), and with the help of the sexton, a crotchety, lovable but slightly dotty octogenarian, endeavors to save the church building from the evil forces of progress. The building loses, the ghost fades, but the apostolic tradition endures. The deacon in the novel symbolizes two values in the parish, mediation and continuity. He is "a bridge figure," ordained yet remaining a layman in lifestyle, who over the years has become "a listening post for many," especially the old. He is also permanent. "A priest can be replaced; a deacon, in evidence at the same altar for twenty, thirty, forty years, assisting so many people, cannot."

But not all the perpetual deacons still active are as content and loved as Gard was. Many are unhappy, feeling rejected by the church and betrayed by changes that have left them marooned in the past. A few years ago I received a sad letter from an elderly deacon in Tennessee, whose wife had died, and who lamented, "They have taken away my ministry!" He meant that he could no longer pass the chalice, for his rector had given *his* chalice to licensed chalice-bearers to administer. The church had given the deacon no support in the loss of his wife or his ministry, and made no effort to help him in his old age find new service in the new age.

Sometimes deacons' unhappiness is their own fault. One criticism of perpetual deacons was their occasional excess of sacramental zeal. The 1928 Prayer Book of the Episcopal Church, whatever its historic and literary virtues, was strangely mute about diaconal liturgy, so deacons had to invent a good deal. In most places perpetual deacons officiated at the "deacon's mass"—a public communion service using the reserved sacrament (for which there was no rubrical provision)—and some deacons went so far as to say part of the eucharistic prayer, sometimes stopping after the Sanctus, sometimes omitting only the words of institution. To bring order out of disorderly behavior, the 1979 Book of Common Prayer provided rubrics for such a liturgy and required the deacon to omit the entire eucharistic prayer and fraction. Many older deacons mistakenly think of the "deacon's mass" as a regular form of liturgy, rather than as an emergency feeding from the cupboard.

Other critics have charged that perpetual deacons were trying to take a shortcut into the priesthood. Indeed, some did go on to priestly orders, as the canon permitted. Without tracking the biographical records of all 517 perpetual deacons ordained in 1952 through 1970, it is hard to tell exactly how many became priests. An inspection of the published ordination reports indicates that only four became priests within a year or two of their deaconing. Others became priests years later, mainly during the tumultuous 1970s. Who knows how many! Given the large number of perpetual deacons still alive, I suspect they were few. Let us remember that the bishop allowed them to become priests. Some were missionary or indigenous deacons whom the church intended to make priests. Some changed their mind. Some were persuaded by the bishop or others. A few took the easy path. In main, though, the canon was used for what it was designed, deacons until death.

So let us honor the perpetual deacons. For almost two decades, maybe longer, the church needed them and ordained them. Most of them ministered with dedication and did not aspire to "higher office." They loved the church they served, the people they served, the altar they served. But the need for them passed.

ENDNOTES

1. The concept of the four waves was proposed by James L. Lowery, Jr., in 1979. I have changed his order to put missionary deacons first, since they were the earliest in terms of ordination dates and canonical provision.

2. See Susan Fenimore Cooper, *William West Skiles, a Sketch of Missionary Life at Valle Crucis in Western North Carolina, 1841-1862* (n.p., 1890).

3. See *Oakerhater* (Oklahoma City, Okla.: St. John's Episcopal Church Press, 1982), and Lois Clark, *David Pendleton Oakerhater: God's Warrior* (Oklahoma City: Diocese of Oklahoma, 1985).

4. See Owanah Anderson, *Jamestown Commitment: The Episcopal Church and the American Indian* (Cincinnati: Forward Movement Publications, 1988) pp. 56, 68, 70-71, 79-80, 109, and 128.

5. For the English history, see the ACCM study by Janet Grierson, *The Deaconess* (London: CIO, 1981).

6. Mary P. Truesdell, "The Office of Deaconess," in *The Diaconate Now*, ed. Richard T. Nolan, (Washington, D. C.: Corpus Books, 1968), pp. 158-161.

7. *EWHP Newsletter* 4:1 (Winter 1984), 1; 7:4 (Fall 1987), "For your files" 1; 8:1 (Winter 1988), 7-8. In 1978 the National Center for the Diaconate formed the Deaconess History Project, directed by Kathryn A. Piccard. The project consisted of three parts: a directory of the 450 deaconesses, an archive of deaconess books and other material, and an oral history project, with taped interviews of deaconesses by Piccard and Mary Sudman Donovan, whose book *A Different Call: Women's Ministries in the Episcopal Church, 1850-1920* (Wilton, Conn.: Morehouse-Barlow, 1986), contains information about Episcopal deaconesses.

8. *EWHP Newsletter* 3:4 (Fall 1984), 6.

9. *EWHP Newsletter* 5:4 (Fall 1985), 3; 6:1 (Winter 1986), 8.

10. "Deaconess Harriet Bedell: missionary to the Mikasukis," *The Diocesan* [Diocese of Florida], Advent 1989, p. 9.

11. Material on Nevada deaconesses furnished by Josephine Borgeson. See *Diakoneo* 12:3 (May 1990).

12. Robert E. Gard, *The Deacon* (Madison: R. Bruce Allison Wisconsin Books, 1979).

4

Modern Deacons

*T*he three early waves of the diaconate in the Episcopal Church have all but vanished, as the church's needs for ministry have changed. Mission areas need indigenous priestly leadership, as well as deacons who encourage and lead the people in service. As fully recognized members of an historic order, women are a vital part of the ministry of deacons. The sacramental and pastoral ministries of perpetual deacons have become absorbed in the rising perception of baptismal ministry as the obligation of all the faithful.

The early waves, however, have much to tell us. They teach that leadership in *diakonia* should be local and daring. Like William West Skiles, deacons serve best when they are part of the culture in which they labor. Like David Oakerhater, deacons serve best when they can say, "You all know me, you remember when I . . ." The local Christians should select deacons out of their midst and support them as members of the family with a special role. Like Milnor Jones, deacons serve best when they dare, when they speak out and act out, when they get themselves and others in trouble—even when they arouse the mob.

The early waves teach us, too, that the inclusion of women in holy orders is too important to be compromised and weakened by obsolete attitudes about women's place in church and society. Women have breathed new life into the diaconate. Women deacons have succeeded as outward and visible signs of ministry—especially to the sick and the poor—and a diaconate without women would be incomplete and sadly deprived.

A third lesson we can learn is that close pastoral association with local Christians over a long time benefits both the church and the deacon. In this fickle world we may scorn permanence, but stability strengthens the church—as it does the home and family. The people of God who formerly welcomed the stranger value friendship over estrangement. And the local people are more likely to follow a familiar deacon than a distant one into service in the world.

The 1970s: A transitional decade

In 1971 the Episcopal Church began to ordain what appeared to be a new style of deacon, which was actually an attempt to recover an old style—the classic diaconate of the early church. A few years earlier, in the Roman Catholic Church, Vatican II had called for this recovery in the form of a permanent diaconate, which Paul VI promulgated in 1967. The Lambeth Conference of 1968 had urged Anglican churches to open the order to men and women in ordinary life. Liturgical trial in the Episcopal Church, leading eventually to the 1979 Book of Common Prayer, included deacons and other baptized persons as vital parts of a diversified liturgy. Women could be deacons. Most important of all, the Episcopal Church began to expect deacons to function directly under the bishop as symbols of the servant Christ and as special servants of the poor in the world.

During the same decade, many men used the normal deacon canon to become priests, while many dioceses allowed and even supported this legal but peripheral use of the canon. The 1973-78 bulge in the number of male deacons ordained priests coincided with the movement to ordain women as priests, as well as with a trend toward ordaining older men as priests. Perhaps these men who followed the deacon track to become priests wanted to avoid the economic and social disruption of seminary. Perhaps they lacked confidence in the Episcopal Church's support of its deacons, or perhaps they simply viewed the diaconate as a transitional period and the priesthood as the ordained norm. Or the answer may lie in a complex set of concurrent events. But the trend was disturbing. For six years the Episcopal Church seemed unwilling to order itself for *diakonia*, and in general the ordering of the church itself appeared confused and unruly.

The stories of several deacons ordained during the 1970s, myself among them, illustrate the transitional nature of the diaconate during that decade. We were sometimes confused about what we were and where we belonged. Many of us had to find our own way without the help or guidance of our bishops, who tended to be puzzled by our desire to become deacons. The old perpetual diaconate often cast its shadow over our vocations.

In 1970, under the influence partly of the liturgical movement and partly of the Roman Catholic revival of the order, I applied for the diaconate in the diocese of Louisiana. My bishop, Iveson Noland, who would let people do whatever they wanted so long as it appeared "catholic," cheerfully allowed me to proceed. After a year of solitary "reading for orders" to prepare for canonical examinations, I took the same exams as the seminary graduates. I sat for my formal photograph in clerical dress. At my ordination on 11 July 1971 Bishop Noland stood in the pulpit and addressed me as "Father Plater, the new curate of St. Anna's." (Many older people in the congregation still call me "Father.") The next day, in clericals, I drove to the airport to pick up a visitor, and the parking lot attendant waved me out without payment. A week later I received a clergy discount at a clothing store. But when an Episcopal preparatory school offered me a job as chaplain, members of the board of trustees turned me down on the grounds that I wasn't "fully ordained."

As it has turned out, my ministry as deacon has taken a far different course. It led me first to the local prison, then to hospitals, and most recently to the surgical wards in New Orleans Charity Hospital, where many of the patients are the gunshot and stabbing casualties of urban warfare. In the parish I visit the sick and shut-in, and in the diocese I serve as secretary of the commission on ministry and as a coordinator of lay hospital visiting. Farther afield I have a ministry of editing, writing, and speaking, mostly about deacons. Recently I estimated that I have undergone about ten major changes in ministry in almost twenty years; the bishop called me to about half the changes, and the other half I started on my own. Since I tend to accumulate the ministries I supposedly have moved out of, I may still be a curate.

Perhaps more typical of the transitional decade are the stories of women who either stumbled into or were talked into the diaconate. The path taken by Josephine Borgeson, a seminarian who changed her route from the priesthood to the diaconate, was influenced by chance:

> When I was at seminary, my inner call came through a study of the proposed ordination rites. The phrase "to interpret to the church" really hit me right between the eyes. My call was confirmed through my work with the people of the Diocese of Nevada at our summer camp, Galilee. I was told by women leading the movement for the ordination of women to the presbyterate and the episcopacy that it was pointless to want to be a deacon, because the power in the church lay with being a priest or a lay leader, preferably wealthy. A few professors and

fellow students heard what I was saying about the diaconate, and helped me ground my theology, and create,
in the free wheeling early seventies, a curriculum that
was appropriate to my gifts and vocation.

Borgeson was ordained in 1974 by Wesley Frensdorff,
who put her in charge of ministry development in a
diocese that became famous for its expression of "total
ministry." She remained in that job for fourteen years,
even after the resignation of Frensdorff in 1985, and
then worked for two years as an independent contractor
in diaconal ministries, trying to exercise her gifts of
teaching, administration, and preaching on the margins
of the church and society. In 1990 Borgeson was hired
as Christian education missioner for the diocese of Los
Angeles. "I see servant leadership as focusing on enabling others to serve," she writes, "And I see servanthood
as more a style of ministry than a particular set of duties."

Borgeson recognizes that being a deacon is a risky
business, which not only places the deacon in jeopardy,
but also poses a terrible threat to those who wish to
defend the church as it currently exists. "And whenever
you threaten, you've got to expect some pain, most of it
seemingly undeserved. My problem is, I just don't know
how to do it any differently if Jesus is our example."[1]

In 1977 Borgeson preached at the ordination of
several CDSP graduates, to a congregation including Arlinda Cosby, a seminarian who had begun to feel vo-
cationally different from her classmates. "Her words
seemed to turn on a light bulb somewhere. Eureka!
That's it!" Momentarily stalled by pregnancy and the
birth of a daughter, Cosby graduated and was ordained
in 1979 to find herself with a young child, a permanently disabled husband, and a desire to work in institutions offering long-term care. Her bishop, her

rector, and an archdeacon advised her to forget about earning a living in the church. "One of them said I had three strikes against me: I was a woman, I was a deacon, and I wanted to work with the elderly." She worked for a while as activity director in a convalescent hospital but became frustrated at trying to justify this position as service of Christ.

Eventually, in 1981, the deanery in Alameda, California, hired Cosby to coordinate the ministry of twenty-two congregations to seven thousand patients in nearly a hundred facilities. "My vision these past nine years has been to initiate, support, and strengthen the ministries of our local Episcopal congregations to the convalescent hospitals in their communities, offering training, education, support to clergy and the laity, and pastoral care for families and staff as well as patients." In this position, paid the diocesan minimum for a vicar, Cosby works hard to satisfy overwhelming needs, often despairs over the dearth of volunteers, and tries to develop some kind of relationship with the three parishes in which she functions liturgically. She does not feel close to the other deacons of the diocese, most of whom are graduates of the diocesan School for Deacons, which troubles her at times. "Feeling neither fish nor fowl has become a familiar feeling over the past 11 years—perhaps it's only what life on the diaconal edge is all about."

Around 1972, David W. Brown, a priest in Vermont, suggested to his parishioner Jean Brooks that she become a deacon. At first she regarded him as mildly deranged, but the idea kept re-surfacing, and "it dawned on me that this invitation might be a way that God had prepared for me to return thanks for a long ago life-changing conversion experience." Her bishop, also skeptical but "willing to be shown," ordained her in 1979.

I myself couldn't be very persuasive on the matter since I had scarcely any idea what a deacon was or did. My preparation did nothing to enlighten me about the diaconate, since it was not designed for that purpose. After three years of preparation and taking the General Ordination Examinations, I made my final appearance before the Commission on Ministry. When asked what I expected to be doing as a deacon, I recall that my answer was: "I suppose I will be doing whatever David tells me to do." I don't think anyone on the Commission had any more idea about diaconal ministry than I did, in fact possibly less, and I suppose I sounded nicely biddable, so they passed me on.

Her experience as a deacon has been "a continuous unfolding of opportunities for learning and service," all arising from needs unrelated to any structure or regulation. She cares for the parish needy, administers a discretionary fund, and in her outreach to the community has been involved in organizations related to the hungry, the developmentally disabled, emotionally disturbed children and adults, and prisoners. She often involves "eager and dedicated young people in these situations."

The decade of the 1970s was also a time of serious canonical revision in attempts to bring about reform. Thus in 1970 General Convention enacted significant changes in the old perpetual deacon canon, resulting in a new canon that begins:

A man of Christian character, proven fitness, and leadership in his community, who is willing to serve in the capacity of Deacon without relinquishing his secular occupation, may be proposed and recommended to the Bishop, for enrollment as a Postulant, by the Minister and Vestry of the Parish in which his service is desired . . . . [III.10.10(a)]

It was intended as a canon that would help restore the diaconate as a permanent order with local ties. Originally intended to provide for deacons only, it was afterwards expanded to provide for subsequent ordination to the priesthood. Alaska and similar dioceses with remote and ethnic congregations needed local priests, or sacramentalists (as they were then called), and canon III.10.10 seemed the easiest way to get them.

The canon also required a major change in practice, for prospective deacons were no longer to apply on their own initiative. Under the canon a qualified person is to be "proposed and recommended to the Bishop" by a parish, mission, or diocesan body. This provision was intended to shift the emphasis on God's call from the person to the community, from the inner call to the outer call. The proposed deacon must be willing (although not required) to remain in secular work. Although a few deacons ordained under this canon have received stipends from the church, at least for part-time work, most have remained non-stipendiary.

Several important amendments were made over the next nine years. In 1973 the paragraph on preparation for ordination was amended to introduce some flexibility, and consequently preparation was divided into two equal parts, academic and practical, thus shifting the emphasis from solely academic study (often modeled after seminary preparation) to include practical training and recognition of the value of practical experience in *diakonia*. The canon also required "an evaluation of the Candidate's attainments" instead of the usual formal examinations. The sum of these changes implied a new kind of deacon, formed more in the hospitals, prisons, and soup kitchens than in the study hall.

As in the early church, deacons are subject to the bishop. The bishop assigns them, and they cannot accept work in another diocese without the consent of the bishops of both dioceses. Unfortunately, the canons assumed that all deacons are the same, as though there were no difference between "permanent" and "transitional" deacons, although trends in the diaconate were leading toward two distinctive types of deacons.

The 1970s were a decade of severe change, years of uncertainty, upheaval, and often chaos. Many in the church held desperately to old and tried ways, while others were eager to try anything new. The resulting tumult applied to orders as well as to liturgy and other aspects of church life. Until the 1980s few bishops and commissions on ministry took seriously either the canonical requirement that deacons be "proposed and recommended" or the requirement for practical training. For a few years the revival of the diaconate seemed in danger of collapse, and confusion about the role of the deacon was a large part of the problem.

After 1979 the transitional period ended. Holy orders began to recover a measure of harmony, and service of "the poor, the weak, the sick, and the lonely," as the prayer book directed, rose in significance as the distinguishing mark of the diaconate. The new Book of Common Prayer assigned deacons a central role in the life of the church. Canon III.10.10 began to be used for what it was primarily intended—the ordination of deacons who would remain in the order.

During these same years the deacons of the Episcopal Church and their friends built an organization. After 1970 the Central House for Deaconesses, located in an old house at 1914 Orrington Avenue in Evanston, Illinois, lost its purpose as a training center for women. Its director, Frances Zielinski, a former deaconess become deacon, decided to expand the organization to include men deacons. In 1974 the board of trustees, which now included several men deacons as well as women deacons, changed the name to the National Center for the Diaconate.

The center had a troubled start. One problem was lack of money, another was lack of energy and direction. Semi-annual meetings were poorly attended, brief, and listless. Trustees traveled often hundreds of miles to attend meetings one to two hours long. Projects were vague and seldom carried out. Some board members complained. Some stayed away. The center had little sense of what to do. Its one important activity in the mid-1970s was a survey of some thousand deacons (permanent and transitional) over two years. The survey found that deacons whose diaconate centered on the altar tended to feel frustrated and as a result often sought the priesthood. By contrast those whose diaconate centered on ministry to the poor and needy tended to feel fulfilled and excited and were content to remain deacons.

The first new work, approved in 1977, was the Deaconess History Project, a worthwhile activity which needed support but which turned out to be a major drain on funds. The second was a small newsletter, *Diakoneo*, which in 1978 began to be published quarterly and mailed free to deacons and friends.

The turning point can be traced to the efforts of two people. One was James L. Lowery, Jr., a priest in Boston, who for six and a half years traveled the country in the course of his work and spoke to diocese after diocese about his theory of the four waves of the diaconate. He also described the basic four-part design of a diaconate program: selection, training, deployment, and supervision and support. The other friend was Wesley Frensdorff, bishop of Nevada. When Frensdorff joined the board in 1978, the center began to come alive. At his second meeting he started a discussion about the theology of the diaconate, and the meeting lasted an unprecedented five hours. Frensdorff expressed his dream of a deacon in every parish as an outward and visible sign of servant ministry and as an enabler of the ministry of all the baptized.

Elected president in 1983, Frensdorff brought several strengths to the center. One was a theological approach. He argued that deacons are not merely functionaries; they fill a sacramental role as symbols or icons of Christ. Another strength was experience. Frensdorff had already put into practice in Nevada his concept of "total ministry," whereby a parish or mission organizes itself for the ministry of all the baptized. Total ministry includes selection by the congregation, from its members, of its priest and deacon—perhaps several of each.

The National Center for the Diaconate continued to be plagued by financial setbacks. Out of a desire to include the Anglican Church of Canada, which was seeking to renew the diaconate, the North American Association for the Diaconate came into being in 1986 as its replacement. One activity of both organizations was to hold or cosponsor conferences. The first three, in 1979, 1981, and 1984, were characterized by the uncertainty over the diaconate which still was widespread in the Episcopal Church.[2] Many deacons and persons in the application process came to the conferences seeking emotional support. Some shared tales of woe, others were in pain over what they perceived as their bishops' neglect. At the 1984 conference several deacons openly disagreed over the propriety of clerical dress for their order. Some opposed clerical dress and titles for deacons. Some defended the clerical collar. More in tune with the aggressive new style of deacon, as with the American trait of self-reliance, was a motto suggested at the 1981 meeting by William B. Arnold, a deacon in Central Florida: "Don't ask, do it!" The motto also suggested a mood of rebellion against bishops.

A similar mood characterized the 1987 conference on the diaconate held in Kansas City, Missouri. The Presiding Bishop of the Episcopal Church, Edmond L. Browning, pledged to encourage the diaconate in the Episcopal Church, but also challenged deacons to articulate and model diaconal ministry, to join him in making the church inclusive, and to re-examine the spiritual basis of their ministry. In the question session next day, however, Browning faced heavy opposition from several deacons and others to the continued use of the transitional diaconate—what one deacon called "climbing up a ladder." Browning argued in return that the transitional diaconate should be emphasized as "a spiritual moment in the life of a person who's come into the ordained ministry," and this depiction of permanent office as a fleeting experience stirred up a nest of hornets. Sarah Tracy, who forms deacons in Northern Indiana, charged, "The deacon, the honest-to-God deacon, is trained to be a deacon. The transitional deacon is trained to be a priest, and they are giving *diakonia* a bad name."[3]

Another organization involved in the renewal of the diaconate has been Associated Parishes for Liturgy and Mission. Founded in 1946, in its early years Associated Parishes campaigned for catholic liturgical principles, especially the recovery of the eucharist as the central act of Christian worship. In the late 1970s the council of the organization turned its attention to the diaconate and issued the Wewoka Statement calling for

> the renewal of the order of deacons as a full, normal ministry in the Church, alongside the priesthood. The diaconate is not properly a stepping-stone or a back door to the priesthood. It is not an auxiliary ministry. Deacons and priests have equal but different ministries whose functions are clearly outlined in the new ordinal of the Proposed Book of Common Prayer.

The council also urged that candidates be ordained directly to the priesthood, without an intervening transitional diaconate, and that deacons "be eligible to be elected as bishop and ordained directly to that order."[4] This was the main issue raised by the Wewoka Statement—*per saltum* ("by a leap"), or direct ordination, the ancient practice of ordaining a person directly to the order intended. Despite the extensive overhaul of the canons on ministry in 1988, the canon on ordination to the priesthood still requires prior ordination to the diaconate. The Episcopal Church thus leaves unresolved one of its greatest contradictions. The 1979 Book of Common Prayer makes no mention of holding, or remaining in, a prior order, and all ordinands approach the bishop vested in a white garment without stole or vestment of office. The symbolism of the liturgy thus says that instead of asserting prior office (whether they continue in one or not is unclear), they come to ordination simply as baptized persons.

Maturity in the 1980s

The 1980s were a time of increased public discussion of the order. James M. Barnett's scholarly study *The Diaconate: A Full and Equal Order* in 1981 helped the church take the diaconate seriously as a permanent order of ministry in the world. Furthermore, through its revision of the canons on ministry, the Episcopal Church has begun to separate the diaconate from the priesthood. But only in part. The process for recruitment and selection, postulancy, and candidacy is shared, without distinction, by deacons and priests. The former description of a deacon's qualifications—"A person of Christian character, proven fitness, and leadership in his community"—no longer appears in the canons, while the "proposal" process of the old deacon canon now applies to both deacons and priests. The emphasis for both orders is now on recruitment and selection: bishops and priests are "to identify fit persons" and encourage them to apply, although how this is to happen is not spelled out. The main difference still lies in formation and in the final steps of the ordination process. Formation is still divided into two parts, academic and practical. Deacons are assigned to a parish or mission "at the request, or with the consent," of the rector and vestry. A deacon who moves to another diocese may be given a "license" to function as deacon only on the written request of the bishop, with the written consent of the standing committee. By the end of the decade, deacons in the Episcopal Church numbered 1,275—789 men and 486 women—with about 400 people in training.

Deacons and priests ordained in the 1980s appear more willing than those ordained earlier to accept the argument that *diakonia* is acquired primarily in baptism, and that whereas the ordained diaconate may be a canonical requirement, it is not a theological, historical, or practical prerequisite for the ordained priesthood. In the mind of deacons, at least, the distinction between deacon and priest grows clearer.

A story told by the Canadian deacon Maylanne Whittall at the 1989 conference at Kanuga shows a change in the nature of deacons. A woman on the bank of a river sees someone drowning. The woman jumps in and saves the person. A few minutes later, she sees someone else drowning and jumps in again. This happens again, and it happens a few more times. Finally the woman walks away, and the crowd which has gathered asks where she is going. "You can't leave these people to drown!" She answers, "I'm going up the river to see who's throwing them in."

Deacons ordained in the 1980s tend to look for the sources of drowning; some of them have also experienced it. One of these is Marcos Rivera, ordained in Central Florida in 1987. Two years later he attended an ecumenical conference on *diakonia* in Kingston,

Jamaica, of which he wrote: "My native background and lifestyle in a tropical area did little to prepare me for the food delicacies, weather, scenery, and breathtaking beauty of Jamaica. Neither was I prepared for the poverty in such a beautiful place." Rivera comes from a background that is exotic in its own way. Born in Puerto Rico in 1939, he grew up in the slums of New York, where he became a heroin addict and for thirteen years was a member of street gangs. Then, converted to Christ, spiritually and physically delivered from gang violence, street life, and drug dependence, he left New York, attended college in Ohio, founded three homes for boys there, and eventually settled in Florida. In 1974 he set up Anchor House, a home for neglected and abused boys, which he still runs as executive director. Rivera travels extensively to speak about the home and raise money, and also works for an Episcopal parish in Lakeland, Florida, as a paid assistant in charge of missions and family development.

At the Jamaica meeting, attended mostly by deaconesses and other women from protestant churches, Rivera listened while speaker after speaker talked about God as a woman and prayed to God as "Mother." Finally he rose and told the audience that street people like him were not interested in the sex of God, or even in God. Later a group of women followed him out of the hall and thanked him for his comments.

Rivera has a strong sense of the power of Christ to change lives and of the presence of Christ in men, women, and children suffering from poverty. Like Francis of Assisi, he often finds in a commonplace experience the dramatic physical evidence of God. "While walking inside a mission for the handicapped," he writes of his Jamaican trip, "I was approached by a young woman of indeterminable age. She grabbed my hand and kissed it. As she kissed my hand, she also reached and hugged me. I felt a fiery sensation through my entire body. I have never been a mystic, but when she hugged me I felt as though I was being hugged by the Lord. A transformation occurred within me."5

Justus Van Houten came home from Vietnam in 1973 with a desire to become a Franciscan friar. At the time he felt that the vocation of friar was incompatible with the vocation of deacon (although Francis of Assisi had been a deacon). In the early 1980s, after ten years as a friar, he changed his mind and with the support of his brothers was ordained at the annual chapter of the Society of St. Francis in 1986, as the society's first deacon friar. "The community felt that it needed to have the servant aspect of their ministry sacramentalized."

For the first two years of his diaconate, Brother Justus worked for the San Francisco Night Ministry, a job that entailed spending Saturday nights on the streets, in bars and coffee shops, and other places where people hang out. He helped and befriended robbed tourists, stranded people, patients who had lost their medication, recovering alcoholics, potential suicides, and the like. One night the patrons of a seedy gay bar decided to stage a drag show to cover the burial expenses of "Diane," a bartender who had died from AIDS. Justus attended as a sign of the church's official presence at a community enterprise. When the sound system failed to arrive, the crowd became restless and he was asked to do a memorial service. "I talked about love. The love that was so obvious for so many people to have come out to raise money for Diane's burial, and that while I didn't know Diane's religious background, that as a Christian who believed in a God of love, that this outpouring of love helped me to have a deeper understanding of God as I knew him. We ended with a toast to Love and passed the hat."

Some weeks later, during a routine visit at the county jail, an inmate told Justus that the service for Diane had been his first encounter with a church that did not judge and condemn him. The inmate was later baptized in the jail, "quite a courageous act on his part."

Montie Slusher retired in 1990 as a teacher with the North Slope Borough School District in Barrow, on the Arctic coast of Alaska, and moved inland to Fairbanks. His ministry in one of the coldest and remotest parts of the continent began with his arrival in 1969 to work with the poor and those who needed education and vocational training. Raised as a Methodist, he attended a nearby Episcopal church, was confirmed, and served as lay reader and senior warden. "The deacons' charge 'to interpret to the church the needs of the world' was very real to me, as I worked with those who had such needs." As school principal in the small village of Point Lay, where about half the 120 residents were Episcopalians, he learned more about the diaconate and was ordained in 1985.

Slusher plans to spend his retirement working as a deacon. The bishop asked him to put his experiences as social worker, educator, and vocational trainer into writing grants and training local people for native ministries in the interior and Arctic coast. This direction from his bishop is important to Slusher, who believes that "diaconal ministry is only possible with the guidance of the bishop." His background as teacher and deacon also leads him to emphasize the connection between ordinary life and the church. He writes:

> The deacon's journey is not an upward movement, but rather one of lateral movement into the world of people. The deacon must lead others from worship back into the day-by-day realities all must face in the world. If a deacon feels he has "arrived," he will become frustrated or worse yet, stale. The role of the deacon is to see that

the drawbridge is always open allowing entry into the castle and that two way traffic is possible allowing entry into the castle (church) and to lead others back into the world.

In 1982, four months after ordination, Shep Jenks quit his job and, surviving on Navy retirement pay, went to work as a deacon in the diocese of California. He describes the changes that have followed:

> I was assigned first to one mission church and then to another where my bishop felt that help was needed. I worked hard and did well. I was really filling a position as an unpaid curate (or assistant vicar). I was on a high. My prayer life was good. I read and studied Holy Scriptures regularly. I had recovered from a divorce and found Nancy, who is a born servant. I had a disagreement with the vicar and handled it poorly. I had to be right. The naval officer (and all the power that entailed) came out.

The bishop moved Jenks into San Francisco to help at Canon Kip Community Center, where he ended up as executive director, unpaid, working overtime, "and thoroughly rewarded personally as Nancy's and my new ministry flourished." Having started as a curate, he now felt that deacons should be "down in the bowels of the inner city." When they moved to Hawaii to be with Nancy's aging father, they discovered that support of the diaconate in Hawaii had dwindled. Jenks decided to remain a canonical resident of California. Although they attended a parish with a sympathetic rector and worked at a shelter for the homeless, where Jenks was on the board of directors, they were heartbroken when they saw the low spirits of the remaining deacons in Hawaii. After his sometimes joyful, sometimes painful experiences in change of ministry and diocese, Jenks is convinced that a deacon must serve in both the church and the world.

I now feel that a deacon can best serve (as a symbol of the need for a servant church) when the person serves in the world but with the laity of a parish/mission. It is most discouraging to be in a place where either priests and bishops can do it all or in which the need for servanthood is not envisioned.

Gloria E. Wheeler, ordained in Central Florida in 1983, has developed a ministry of healing, which includes the personal experiencing of miracles as a result of the power of prayer. But her work as deacon has also ranged from "balancing checkbooks for the aged to emptying urinals for a bedridden bishop." Her husband Robert strongly supports her ministry, which involves being a woman deacon in a conservative diocese. When she was seeking ordination in her parish, the Cathedral of St. Luke in Orlando, "it was then ludicrous to even think of women in the sanctuary unless they were Altar Guild members." One result of her visibility as a deacon has been the opening up of opportunities for ordained women in the diocese.

Jeffrey Ferguson of Maine found her ministry undergoing a drastic change during the process leading to ordination in 1985. She first envisioned herself as a parish assistant, working with young persons and perhaps visiting in nursing homes, but while taking clinical pastoral education in preparation for the diaconate she found herself in a prison for men. "From the moment I entered the gates for my interview I knew I was where I belonged." There she stayed for six years as an assistant chaplain, visiting inmates twelve hours a week.

What a growing period this was for me. The inmates challenged me daily with questions about Scripture, God, sin, Satan, and Jesus. They pushed me to read and study the Bible as I had never done in order to be able to talk with them. They brought out my ignorance of our judicial, educational, and welfare systems. And they raised the fighter in me. I'm slowly but surely becoming a challenger of each of these services or systems. . . . The inmates challenged me to enter their pain and sorrow. This put a large burden on me as I had always kept my emotions under control, to myself. As I learned to enter their world I found myself freed to share my own pain and more especially my joy in the gifts of God. This too was a turning point for many of the men when they realized that other people too, perhaps especially chaplains, had pains and sorrows and yet could meet our Lord with joy.

In 1989 Ferguson's ministry took another direction. When she told her bishop that she was ready to leave prison work, he assigned her to move three hundred miles to the northernmost county of Maine, form a cluster council for five churches, and act as a consultant in the search for a priest. A year later, the task was complete and she returned home. Ferguson also coordinates the deacons of the diocese. She finds that after five years as a deacon, "I walk more closely with our Lord and speak of him more often and more freely. I believe I am more adept at noticing hidden emotions, particularly pain, sorrow, and anger. The Holy Bible has become a never ending source of information, anecdotes, refreshment, and renewal as I become more familiar with it. I find joy in all my work even as I steel myself to speak out about injustice and abusive behavior." As she nears her seventieth year she wonders how the Lord will challenge her next.

Lynn Ramshaw, a divorced parent raising three children in Florida, was a social worker who wanted to go to seminary. Her bishop allowed her to enter an experimental training class for the diaconate. A tragedy occurred in one of the families she had rejected as "ineligible" for financial aid; the father was shot and killed while trying to rob a convenience store. Now the family was "eligible." Ramshaw recalls, "I hated all that, told my parish—they responded by establishing the first TRUE fund (Toward the Relief of Urgent Emergencies). There are now more than forty such funds in southeast Florida working in cooperation with local and state service agencies to aid those in legitimate need, but ineligible."

In 1980 she was ordained deacon and continued in social work for the state. Two years later Bishop Calvin Schofield of Southeast Florida hired her as a full-time assistant to develop a social concerns program for the diocese. In 1987 she moved to St. Benedict's Church in Plantation, Florida, as a full-time deacon with the assignment of enabling the ministry of the laity. In 1990 she moved again, to become a full-time student for a year. "I hope, at the conclusion of this part of my journey, to be a part of a qualitative, church-based center for the homeless; I pray also to continue my work as counselor/spiritual director for those seeking to serve."

Bonnie Polley describes herself as "a Cajun living in Glitter Gulch." As a child growing up in Lake Charles, Louisiana, she liked to visit her daddy's law office next door to the jail, stand outside looking up at the men in the jail window, and tell herself, "If only those people had anybody to talk to they would probably not be so bad." As a grownup in Las Vegas, Nevada, she went inside the county jail and listened. Her parish called her to the diaconate, and she was ordained in 1982. As a deacon she interprets to the church the needs, concerns, and hopes of those in jail. The needs vary widely.

> I might find myself cashing checks, picking up mail, contacting a family member, providing reading glasses, replacing a hearing-aid battery. The list of requests is endless. The funniest request I think I ever had was to go and feed this man's horse that had been left out in the desert when the man was arrested. In asking partic-

ulars about the situation, the man told me that the horse was afraid of people, would bite, and that was why he could not get his friend to go feed him. I asked him how he could be sure that the horse would not bite me and his reply was that I had a direct line upstairs. I said that I wondered if the horse knew that. The end result was that we found someone to take care of the horse and the man was relieved of his anxiety about his horse. With tears in his eyes the man told me that there really must be a God because I cared enough to help him, and if I cared then maybe God cared.

One of only a handful of persons ever to enter seminary for the diaconate, Vicki Black found that Nashotah House helped to confirm her calling. It also helped her "to understand that God was calling me to be a deacon who worked in cooperation with people in different yet equal ministries, and not 'just a deacon,' assisting a priest in his or her more elevated calling within a hierarchical order of ministries." Following her ordination in 1987, her bishop assigned her to a parish, put her in charge of retreats and conferences at DeKoven Center, and asked her to help administer the new catechumenal process in the diocese.

At the conference center I see my diaconal ministry more as one of "making things possible for others," much as a household servant assumes certain tasks which free the householders to do the things they need to do. There I also listen to the needs of others, trying to develop conferences and retreats which might address those needs in the light of the gospel, and then providing the space and welcome for people to gather, and hopefully encounter God in their midst in a new way.

In the midst of making phone calls, typing schedules, welcoming guests, publishing brochures and newsletters, and assisting in liturgies, Black struggles to balance frantic activity with authentic ministry. She finds time to hold up "the importance of spirituality to an institutional church which in its rush towards programming has all too often lost its ability to value spiritual growth as an essential aspect of the Christian life." She searches for a spirituality of servanthood in a culture which "tells us (especially women) that we are to 'set our boundaries,' not to let others take advantage of us, not to accept menial tasks unless others are doing as many of those tasks as we are." And while doing all this at DeKoven, in her parish she works hard to proclaim the gospel, listen to the world, and encourage others in their spiritual growth and ministries.

These stories of deacons in the 1970s and 80s illustrate an ordained ministry in the process of evolution. The modern deacon saves the drowning but also finds the causes and tells the church about them, returning to the gathered people of God and around the altar enacting the diaconal ministry. While serving the poor in the broadest sense, this deacon also seeks to define the diaconate in terms an expanded ministry of action, word, and liturgy, functioning within the local people of God and in close cooperation with the bishop of the diocese. It is clear that for many deacons the encouragement, guidance, and direct involvement of their bishop has become a highly important factor in their ministry.

ENDNOTES

1. The deacons' stories in this chapter are all drawn from personal correspondence, and I thank them for permission to quote from their letters.

2. "Proceedings: The Diaconate" (Papers delivered at Conference on the Diaconate, Notre Dame, Ind., 1979), mimeo-

graphed (Boston: National Center for the Diaconate, 1979), and "Summary and Selected Proceedings: Second National Conference on the Diaconate, May 21-23, 1981," mimeographed (Boston: National Center for the Diaconate, 1981). For the major papers delivered at the three conferences, see J. Robert Wright, "The Emergence of the Diaconate," *Liturgy: Diakonia* 2:4 (Fall 1982), 17-23, 67-71; John E. Booty, "The Church as Servant," *Open*, Oct. 1981, pp. 4-10; and Durstan R. McDonald, "Thoughts on the Diaconate," *Open*, Oct. 1984, pp. 6-15.

3. Browning's speech and dialogue on the transitional diaconate are printed in *Diakoneo* 9:2 (Summer 1987), 2-7, 13-15.

4. *Open*, June 1977, p. 1.

5. *Diakoneo* 11:5 (Nov. 1989), 1-2.

5

Ecumenism and the Diaconate

*T*he four waves in the Episcopal Church constitute one small part of the revival of the diaconate in the whole church. In Canada and the rest of the Anglican communion outside North America, and in other places and churches, the revival takes a different but related shape. Above all else it includes the experience and witness of several Roman Catholic priests imprisoned in Germany during World War II. Their reflection on the consequences of war and extermination has influenced the revival of diaconal ministry in many churches besides their own.

The revival of the diaconate in the mid-twentieth century began in cell block 26 of Dachau concentration camp. Roman Catholic priests, including Wilhelm Schamoni, and other Christian clerics interned there began to discuss secretly and at great risk how to revitalize the church after the war so that it would serve a crushed and defeated people in Europe. Their vision included the diaconate. Schamoni kept a written record of their discussions. His notes were smuggled out of the camp, and in 1947 Otto Pies, another priest in the camp, referred to them in an article. Fuller accounts were published later.[1]

These Dachau conversations had a profound effect on the Roman Catholic Church. In 1951 a young forest ranger, Hannes Kramer, formed the first *Diakonatskreis* (diaconate circle) of social workers in Freiburg who felt called to the diaconate, including their wives and fiancés. Other circles were formed in Germany and elsewhere, attracting the support of the theologian Karl Rahner, among others. After further public discussion and writing, Vatican II approved the proposal and Paul VI instituted the permanent diaconate. In a speech in the Vatican council, on 9 October 1964, Cardinal Léon Suenens stressed the sacramental character of the diaconate as stemming from "supernatural realism" and added: "This grade seems to have been set up especially to provide direct help for the bishop in the care of the poor and the proper direction of the community," mainly in brotherly love and the breaking of the bread. He recommended that men already serving in diaconal ministries be ordained deacons.[2] By the end of 1989 there were 15,775 Roman Catholic permanent deacons in the world, all men, most of them married, with 9,250 in the United States. The Roman Catholic revival of the order is a vital part of the background of the revival in some of the Anglican churches.

As the permanent diaconate of the Roman Catholic Church has developed over more than twenty years, its diocesan programs have adhered closely to the magisterium, or teaching authority of bishops, as declared in the decrees of Vatican II, papal statements, and national guidelines. In the United States the permanent deacons, with their large numbers, have made many contacts with Episcopal deacons, and these connections are beneficial to both sides. Although in some dioceses with a severe shortage of priests some Roman deacons are used mainly as pastoral assistants, most Roman and Episcopal deacons share a strong commitment to works of mercy and justice in the world. Episcopal deacons bring to the dialogue the experience of women as deacons, while Roman deacons bring the insight that one is just as much a deacon at home and on the job as in church on Sunday.

The main differences between the Roman and Episcopal diaconate lie in the area of marriage and women. The Roman permanent diaconate is solely for men, and mainly for married men. Their wives usually take part in their training, approve and confirm their ordination, and often join their ministry as half of a diaconal team. Out of this union between orders and marriage has risen a theological concept in which the two sacraments intertwine. A wife extends her husband's diaconate, her husband extends their marriage into his diaconate, and thus the symbolic representation of Christ is multiplied. "A married diaconate takes people who in marriage have been successful at imaging the unity of Church and Christ and ordains them as other Christs."[3] But those who see marriage as a diaconal strength also tend to deplore the exclusion of women from the order. In early 1990 Archbishop Raymond Hunthausen of Seattle halted plans to form a new group of permanent deacons until the role of women in the church is clarified. (The exclusion of women from the Roman diaconate is a matter of discipline rather than theology.) His controversial decision, which was repeated in another diocese, was widely noted and discussed in the Episcopal Church.

The Roman Catholic concept of a married diaconate has linked hands with the Episcopal concept of women deacons in at least two instances. In Rochester, New York, Episcopal deacon Lynne McNulty is married to Brian McNulty, a Roman deacon. With volunteers from their two parish churches, Lynne and Brian work at Elisha House, a home for the dying, where Lynne functions as director. The other example is in Lexington, Kentucky, where Nancy Barton is married to James Barton, a permanent deacon.

Roman Catholic deacons are found in all the familiar areas of care for the poor and needy. They visit in hospitals and prisons, they feed the hungry and house the homeless, and they serve in parish liturgies. Roman deacons also tend to emphasize two forms of *diakonia*, one closely related to family life and the other to professional life. Dennis Scanland of Detroit discovered his ministry after he and his wife Jo Ann suffered through two miscarriages and the crib-death of their infant son. Through his job as assistant manager of a funeral home, Scanland began to reach out to others coping with death and dying. What had been a job became a ministry, which eventually led to ordination in 1984. The archdiocese assigned him to direct its Refugee Resettlement Office, an assignment he found closely linked with his grief work. "I was dealing with loss constantly. These refugees didn't leave their native countries because they wanted to—they had to. There was pain, disillusion, separation." Today Scanland works as a grief therapist at a funeral home. When his father died of cancer, this painful ordeal led him to concentrate on each family's experience of death. He thanks God for making him a good listener to elderly men and women, widows and widowers, and for giving him a loving and faithful wife.[4]

The diaconate of Charles Clough is deeply immersed in the business world. As the chief investment strategist for Merrill Lynch brokerage house, working in what some think is the global center of greed, Clough decides how to allocate portfolio assets. He is continually required to wrestle with the conflicts between Christian ethics and Wall Street practices. Assigned to a parish in West Concord, Massachusetts, he regards his diaconal vows as extending to his work place. Soon after he joined Merrill Lynch in 1987, the giant firm was rocked by a trading scandal involving mortgage-backed securities. As part of his job, Clough helped to alert the company to the liquidity perils involved in real estate. To those who ask what on earth a deacon is doing on Wall Street, he replies: "Wall Street is a center of immense power and with its control of vast capital flows, a potential for good. I see no conflict in a parish deacon working on Wall Street."[5]

One mark of the Roman Catholic Church in the United States has been the willingness of its bishops to move deacons into positions of administrative responsibility. Deacons serve as directors of diaconate programs in several dioceses, and the last two executive directors of the Bishops' Committee on the Permanent Diaconate, headquartered in Washington, D.C., have been deacons Samuel M. Taub and Constantino J. Ferriola, Jr. Another deacon, Robert Balderas, was appointed in 1990 as national director of the Apostleship of the Sea, which oversees Catholic port chaplains (some of whom are deacons) and maritime centers around the country.

The Anglican Communion

In the Anglican communion parallel but less dramatic influences have been at work. The first official expression of interest came as early as 1878 from the West Indian bishops, who suggested the possibility of deacons who remained in secular calling, and whose intellectual qualifications were lower than usually required. The feeling at Lambeth 1878 was that this form of the diaconate could be decided adequately only in diocesan or provincial synods. And there the matter rested until after World War II.

Every ten years the bishops of the entire Anglican communion meet at Lambeth Palace, and it was at successive Lambeth conferences that they next took up the question of the diaconate. By the Lambeth meeting of 1958, the Episcopal Church had already revived the diaconate in the form of perpetual deacons. Recognizing this ordained ministry in North America, as well as the growing movement in Roman Catholicism to revive the order, Lambeth 1958 made a tentative approach toward reviving the diaconate on a communion-wide basis.

A committee report, "The Order of Deacon," observed that in recent years the church had tended to emphasize the offices of reader and catechist at the expense of the diaconate. Either there is no place for the deacon, or else Anglicans must "give the office and function of a deacon its distinctive place, not only in the worship, but in the witness of the Church." The committee wanted Lambeth to invite each province in the Anglican communion to discuss a revival of the distinctive diaconate, which then might include some commissioned lay ministries. The ordinal would have to be changed to include part-time workers, and this scheme would bring other legal, canonical, and constitutional difficulties.

On the basis of the committee report, Lambeth passed resolution 88, "The Office of Deacon":

> The Conference recommends that each province of the Anglican Communion shall consider whether the office of Deacon shall be restored to its primitive place as a distinctive order in the Church, instead of being regarded as a probationary period for the priesthood.[6]

By use of the phrase "instead of," the bishops at Lambeth appear to have contemplated *replacing* the transitional diaconate with the order as anciently practiced. As we shall see, Anglican bishops and other representatives later backed away from this radical position.

Support for a restored diaconate was much stronger in 1968. It came initially in the form of a remarkable essay by John Howe, bishop of St. Andrews in Scotland and later secretary general of the Anglican Consultative Council.[7] In his preparatory paper for Lambeth conference 1968, "The Diaconate," Howe begins by reviewing the evidence of the diaconate in the New Testament, early church, and medieval and modern times. His brief historical survey, sound and full of insight, emphasizes the symbolic being of deacons rather than their diaconal functions or clerical status in the community. The responsibility of early deacons to carry humble loads in simple and lowly areas gave them a symbolic place related to Christ. The Seven of Acts 6, and the primitive deacons who followed them, were important not because they were clerics but because they performed humble service. In the early church the deacons even worked "as beachcombers who sought the corpses of mariners and provided decent burial." In time attention to status and liturgical function led to distortion of the diaconate. The medieval diaconate faded because the deacon could not celebrate mass—the distinctive function of the hierarchy in that age—and thus the diaconate had no purpose except as the final step on the road to priesthood. The Reformation did not change the practice of holy orders for the better. (The nineteenth-century revival of the deacon and deaconess in continental Lutheranism was an exception.) Now there is widespread concern to recover what Howe calls "a real diaconate."

In his essay Howe lists several main reasons for interest in the diaconate: criticism of the uses of deacons in the churches today, ecumenical dialogue, merely nominal use of one of the three orders, shortage of clergy, and the need for assistance in the eucharist. Of these reasons only the first three continue to be significant, at least in the Episcopal Church. But Howe cautions against a functional approach—that of setting up a diaconate to relieve a particular need. Instead, restoration should be based on "what the diaconate is and what deacons are for."

Howe places considerable emphasis on Acts 6 as a starting point that emphasizes flexibility, adaptability, God's powerful gift of grace in the ordained ministry, and the need for the church to display support for those carrying particular responsibilities. The present use of the diaconate as a final period before the priesthood receives no sanction from early history, and we should not confuse a transitional period of probation with a permanent order. Howe was one of the first to question those practices of training, status, and function (including collars and titles) that cause the diaconate to resemble the priesthood, observing that deacons must be distinct from both priests and lay ministers and not duplicate the ministry of either. He was also one of the first to challenge the concept of the indelibility of orders: should the diaconate, at least, be indelible and lifelong or erasable and short-term?

Howe suggested three alternative courses of action for Lambeth 1968: (1) discard the diaconate, (2) discard the diaconate as a step to the priesthood but continue study and experiments, or (3) keep the present diaconate and continue to experiment. Howe clearly preferred the third course, and Lambeth 1968 agreed. But he also wanted to go further and identify the diaconate in existing lay ministries—catechists, readers, nurses, welfare workers, and secretaries—not to ordain them, but simply to commission and bless them with the laying on of hands. Training for such deacons would be diverse and appropriate to indivdual ministries. They would be commissioned in a simple service and licensed by the bishop for a specific ministry and term of years. "In most parts of the world, at such a making of deacons, complete simplicity and lack of trappings would be suitable." Howe closes his essay with a sentence that looks ahead to the new style of deacon:

> The familiar accompaniments of ordinations would too readily revive the curse of the diaconate—the withdrawal from the circumstances of lay life, and a restless feeling that it is not reason [*sic*] that they should serve tables, and that the Church should find some other men of good repute to appoint over that business.

Willing to restore the order of deacons, but not to the lengths of declericalization urged by Howe, the bishops at Lambeth 1968 addressed the issue in Resolution 32, "The Diaconate," by recommending, first, that a diaconate combining service of others with liturgical duties be open to men and women in secular occupations, full-time church workers, and those selected for the priesthood. Second, the resolution recommended that the ordinals should be revised to take this new role into account, to remove any suggestion that the diaconate is an inferior order, and to emphasize the elements of *diakonia* in the ministry of bishops and priests.[8]

The official report of Lambeth 1968 expands on this resolution. There the bishops argue that the practice of continuing to use the diaconate as a probationary period for priesthood is an ecumenical embarrassment (probably because it is untrue to Scripture) requiring reform. The diaconate, as part of Anglican tradition, should not be allowed to lapse, but should be given a more significant place within the Anglican communion. The bishops recommend recovery and renewal of the diaconate, which would be open to men and women and would include both those professionally employed by the church and those in secular employment. Candidates for the priesthood should pass through and be part of the diaconate.

The mention in the resolution of "the continuing element of *diakonia* in the ministry of bishops and priests," a seemingly innocent phrase, may cause confusion today. One theological rationale for ordination to the diaconate of those intended for the priesthood has been that ordained priests need to be deacons to possess the fullness of diaconal ministry. Liturgical revision, occurring after 1968, has raised questions about the validity of such argument. Most modern Anglican baptismal rites, including those of the Episcopal Church and the Anglican Church of Canada, make it clear that a Christian receives both priesthood and *diakonia* at baptism. To participate fully in Christian service all you need is to be baptized. The old career path of climbing from one order to another has washed away.

In view of the strong stand taken by Lambeth 1968, there was little left for the next conference to do. Not all the member churches were prompt to act on the ordination of women deacons, however, and Lambeth 1978 thought it desirable to pass a brief resolution on "Women in the Diaconate," which urges member churches to include women in the order.[9] The resolution reflected an action already taken in the General Convention of the Episcopal Church in 1970 (which also revised the canons for the diaconate in general). In the Church of England women were not ordained as deacons until February 1987. Aside from women as deacons, Lambeth 1978 paid no attention to the revival of the diaconate.

Actions on the diaconate were also taken at three meetings of the Anglican Consultative Council, or ACC, which was called into being by Lambeth 1968 and meets every two or three years. The most important of these was the third meeting of the council, known as ACC-3, which took place in 1976 in Trinidad, West Indies, and addressed at length several issues connected with ministry, both that of the whole people of God and that of the ordained. Although the council report confuses "ordained ministry" with "ordained priesthood," it has some good things to say about the need for training priests who will be rooted in the life of the congregations and dioceses. In a section on the diaconate, the report cites with approval Lambeth 1968 and Howe's article, adding:

> We do not think that the making of deacons on a wider scale than hitherto would cause the laity to feel themselves to be released from responsibility to serve as well as to worship. We would therefore see the Diaconate conferred upon men and women who are deeply committed to Christ within the Church, and who are performing a caring and serving ministry in the world in the name of the Church, or who are carrying out a pastoral ministry in the Church.[10]

The council urged that deacons be brought forward by their local priests and congregations, and that the fundamental requirements to be met are "God's grace, man's response, and the people's recognition." It also outlined three questions: (1) Should formal theological training be separated from necessary preparation for the diaconate? (2) Should dress and title distinguish deacons from lay persons? (3) Should the close relationship of the deacon with the bishop be strengthened?

In 1984 the sixth meeting of the council, in Badagry, Nigeria, observed that the order of deacons as commonly practiced "had degenerated into little more than an apprenticeship for priesthood." At the same time, however, it held up the ideal of the diaconate as a ministry to the poor, the sick, and the marginal, exercised directly under the bishop.

Lambeth conference in 1988 produced no resolutions on the diaconate. In one of the four section reports, however, "Mission and Ministry," the bishops included a discussion of the distinctive diaconate that summarizes the deacon's role in this way: "to focus or be a sign of the ministry of servanthood in the church and in the world" and "to remind the whole church that the essence of ministry is service." But the role of the deacon also includes interpreting the needs, concerns, and hopes of the world to the church. The bishops also observed that in provinces which do not ordain women to the priesthood deacons are rarely distinctively diaconal. In these places deacons are trained like priests for a ministry like that of priests.[11]

One of the unrecognized issues of Lambeth and the ACC, as official bodies studying the diaconate and issuing opinions at the highest levels of the Anglican communion, is that no deacons have acted as consultants or written papers on the diaconate for any of the Lambeth conferences issuing reports and resolutions on deacons. Moreover, no deacons have ever sat as members of the ACC or been present as observers at any council meetings.

Despite these limitations in their gathering of data, Lambeth and the ACC have continued to be guided by the call of John Howe for a distinctive diaconate that operates in the church as a symbol of lowly service. Their reports and resolutions have also reflected the experience of many churches that have successfully revived the diaconate during the last two decades.

Other Anglican churches

The revival of the diaconate in the Church of England got off to a shaky start. Howe's essay and the resolution of Lambeth 1968 produced little initial response in England. In 1974 a working party of the Advisory Council for the Church's Ministry (ACCM) advised the church simply to abolish the diaconate, leaving an ordained ministry of bishops and presbyters. (The group wanted to emphasize that service is the work of all the faithful.) General Synod ignored the advice but made no move to revive the diaconate. In 1977, in a change of mind, the Council of the ACCM suggested three options for the diaconate: its continued use as a short stage of preparation for the priesthood, abolition of the order, or an enlargement of the order to include lay workers, deaconesses, and others.

A more positive response began to appear in the Church of England after 1980. In January 1981 a committee of the Deaconess Community of St. Andrew called an ecumenical consultation on the diaconate in London, attended by many who would be involved in the working of the issue through General Synod and by others who were to begin an experiment in the diocese of Portsmouth. In October the House of Bishops published *The Deaconess Order and the Diaconate*; this was the first step in the process that culminated in the Synod's giving final approval in July 1985 to the Deacons (Ordination of Women) Measure. Women were admitted as deacons in 1987—though for many women the diaconate was only a potential transition to priesthood—and in 1988 the House of Bishops received a report recommending a restoration of the order for men and women. By the end of 1989, 756 deaconesses had been ordained deacon, leaving about 150 continuing deaconesses, of whom about 55 were still active. Only seven dioceses had men deacons. Chief of these was Portsmouth, where the bishop, Timothy Bavin, continued a pioneer program begun by his predecessor, Ronald Gordon, with the ordination in 1985 of seven deacons.

Bavin was also the principal author of the 1988 report commissioned by the House of Bishops, *Deacons in the Ministry of the Church*.[12] It surveys the history and current scope of the order, proposes a theology of a distinctive diaconate based on the *diakonia* received in baptism, and explores the future of the order. The report sees deacons as servants to the wider community, enablers of the church, and servants within the church. All their activity is focused in the liturgy, where the deacon "symbolizes in his or her movement between the people and the altar the union of the whole worshipping community." It concludes by recommending that the Church of England encourage men and women to serve in a distinctive diaconate. General Synod merely noted the report, however, and the House of Bishops in 1989 refused to bring forward specific proposals "because of a lack of theological consensus and practical evidence."[13]

To members of the Episcopal Church, the Church of England's official response had a familiar sound, and the English church seemed to be repeating the turbulence of the 1970s a decade later. But there were fundamental differences. In the Episcopal Church many bishops and others regarded the modern history of the diaconate as a heavy load. There was little enthusiasm for the order of deaconesses, whose few remaining members were being cast to the winds, and the church needed to unburden itself of the quasi-priesthood exercised by perpetual deacons. In recent years, however, the Church of England had few men deacons but a large, vital, and respected order of deaconesses. At the end of 1989, there were 31 men and about 1,116 women in the diaconate in England; more than 500 women worked as full-time stipendiary deacons. (A recent poll indicates that about 425 of the current deacons would become priests if they could.) The Episcopal Church thus had little to teach the Church of England beyond the fact that keeping women out of the priesthood harms the diaconate and all other servant ministries.

The one question still to be clarified in England is whether women may become priests. Until General Synod settles this matter, and women deacons make their choice, the diaconate in the Church of England will contain many women who really want to be priests.

Deacons in England now have their own organization. On 29 November 1988 the inaugural meeting of the Diaconal Association of the Church of England (DACE) was held. Unlike the North American Association for the Diaconate, which gives member dioceses the right to elect trustees, DACE consists only of licensed persons — deacons and deaconesses (except for some retired ones), most Church Army workers, and accredited lay workers. The chief voice of the diaconate is that of a scholar and journalist, Sr. Teresa of the Community of St. Andrew, a religious order which has had women deacons (formerly deaconesses) since 1862. She grew up in the Boston area, graduated from Harvard Divinity School, and moved to England, where she became a deaconess. Dressed in her blue habit, and sometimes wearing a helmet and riding a motorcycle, Teresa is a familiar sight and illustrious character in the tough Notting Hill section where the sisters have their convent. In 1981 she organized the ecumenical consultation on the diaconate in London, began the newsletter *Distinctive Diaconate News* and the scholarly series Distinctive Diaconate Studies, and joined the battle that resulted in the ordaining of women deacons. Her newsletter tells everything you want to know about deacons in the Anglican communion and other churches. In addition to news about England, the British Isles, and far-flung provinces, it contains a calendar of events and deacon saints and lists new books and other publications.[14]

Efforts to restore the diaconate have been undertaken in several other churches of the Anglican communion. In Canada, which has only a scattering of deacons, several dioceses are developing programs, and in 1989 the General Synod "commended" a plan to restore the order. In the Province of Southern Africa official permission for a diaconate of men and women was granted in 1983, to be handled by each diocese, but the number of deacons remains small. The bishops hoped for deacons to help the families of those in prison, often the victims of apartheid. The Scottish Episcopal Church approved a diaconate for men in 1965—although few men took advantage of the opportunity—and in 1986 opened the order to women. Several other provinces allow women to be deacons but refuse to allow them to be priests.

Aside from England, Scotland, and Canada, the development of a true diaconate seems most likely in Australia and New Zealand. In Australia a revival of the diaconate is taking place in many dioceses. Melbourne has taken the lead in ordaining men and women deacons, although most of the women actually feel themselves called to the priesthood. Rockhampton, immense in size, has developed a training program and ordains both men and women. The bishop, who actively participates in training and support, sees the modeling of *diakonia* as part of the role of a bishop. Deacons are being ordained also in Sydney, Perth, Canberra, Brisbane, Northern Territory, Tasmania, and Newcastle. In 1990 there were 92 women deacons in 17 dioceses. The Australian Anglican Diaconal Association (AADA), formerly a deaconess fellowship, now is open also to men and women deacons.

The retired New Testament scholar Reginald H. Fuller visited Australia in 1987-88 and found the women deacons "just getting into their stride" in Canberra—but not in the liturgy. His use of a woman deacon in the liturgy created a strong impression, and later in a speech at the diocesan synod he advocated the full liturgical use of deacons. "Unfortunately, my remarks were misunderstood," he later wrote.

> The women deacons present at the Synod thought that I was degrading them by suggesting that they lay the table and wash the dishes! I guess the trouble was that they thought of themselves as transitional deacons who hoped to be advanced to the priesthood. They did not appreciate that it was the dignity of the deacon to serve at table as well as to serve in the world. Unfortunately, I

did not have a chance to explain that this was not a job for female deacons only and that a male deacon, properly used, would do the same chore.[15]

In New Zealand the main changes have been attitudinal rather than structural. One of the few male deacons, Peter Sykes, reports that he wanted to become a deacon "so that I could work in the church's name in the community," but as a compromise he first had to train for the priesthood in seminary. Now the church has begun to awaken. In 1988 a report to the General Synod advocated experimentation with a diaconate of "caring, sacrificial service."

Other Anglican provinces may eventually get around to reviving the diaconate. In 1986 the diocese of Chile proposed reviving the diaconate as a practical ministry—and also proposed ordaining presbyteral candidates directly to the priesthood after a period as a licensed "assistant pastor"—but the province, the Southern Cone of South America, narrowly defeated the motion in synod, largely on the grounds that bishops and priests should never lose sight of their *diakonia*. Several deacons are active in other parts of South America. In the diocese of Ecuador (canonically part of the Episcopal Church) one young deacon, Gonzalo Oñate-Alvarado, lectures on public health in a university, has been a deputy in the national congress, plays a prominent role in the church, and refuses to be ordained priest.

It remains to be said that the revival of the diaconate in Anglican churches has tended to occur at the same time as, or a few years after, renewal of liturgy. Strangely, only a few of the new eucharistic liturgies provide for the use of deacons. The Anglican churches in the United States and Canada give more rubrical instructions than any others, and hence they make fuller provision for deacons in the liturgy. In most other provinces the liturgies scarcely mention deacons. In England and many other countries a reader proclaims the gospel, the intercessions are led by the president or by the minister or leader, and what happens at the preparation of the gifts and at communion is sketched out vaguely, if at all. In many churches the presider says the dismissal. The rubrics, or lack of rubrics, make it possible for anyone, including deacons, to function in the traditional diaconal roles. As Reginald Fuller discovered in Australia, the problem will be to teach and explain the diaconal tradition throughout the Anglican communion.[16]

Fortunately, opportunities for churches to symbolize *diakonia* in the liturgy do not depend on detailed instructions. The spirit of the age embraces freedom and adaptation, rather than restraint and prescription, and these liberal traits will open space in the liturgy for deacons who serve in the world. The general intercessions are an example of liturgy that has been opened up to the people. Over the years forms of prayer have become more flexible and therefore more accessible to a variety of leadership and to congregational participation. The monologues typical of earlier Anglican intercession (including the 1928 Book of Common Prayer of the Episcopal Church) have given way to litanies, to open forms alternating with set texts, to multiple options, to seasonal and occasional prayers, and to prayer that is locally composed and even spontaneous. In many churches it is common for lay persons to create or lead the prayers. As deacons appear more and more in the churches, it will seem right for those who work with the poor and needy to take part, especially to lead, in prayer for them.

Revisions of the ordination liturgy in recent years have also tended to take deacons more seriously. The ordinal of 1550, virtually unchanged except for the revisions of 1662, endured in most Anglican provinces until recent years. In ordaining a deacon, the bishop laid on hands but did not pray, declaring instead: "Take thou Authority to execute the Office of a Deacon in the Church of God committed unto thee; In the Name of the Father, and of the Son, and of the Holy Ghost. Amen" (1928 Prayer Book). The rite nowhere mentioned a bestowal of the Holy Spirit on the candidates. This imperative formula may not have been as defective as it now seems, since Cranmer appears to have believed that deacons already were, as Acts 6:3 says, "full of the Spirit and of wisdom." The apostles simply recognized outwardly what God had already created within persons. In this sense deacons are distinct from bishops and presbyters, who receive the Spirit in a public ceremony, just as Christ bestowed it on his apostles.

In the late twentieth century Anglican churches have abandoned the Cranmerian model and theology of ordination, choosing to follow instead the models of the third and fourth centuries. The typical prayer begins with remembrance of Jesus as servant, who humbled himself and became obedient even to death on a cross, and with thanksgiving for God's call of the deacon. Then the bishop, laying on hands, prays, "Send down the Holy Spirit upon your servant *N.* for the office and work of a deacon in your Church" (Church of England) or some similar invocation. In the 1989 prayer book of New Zealand the ordination prayer reveals a lyric trend in liturgical composition. At the laying on of hands the bishop prays, "God of grace, through your Holy Spirit, gentle as a dove, living, burning as fire, empower your servant *N* for the office and work of a deacon in the Church." At the end the people shout, "Amen! May *they* proclaim the good news, inspire our prayers, and show us Christ, the Servant."[17]

Ecumenical Trends

If the ecumenical movement sometimes stumbles over priests and bishops, it strides easily among deacons. Deacons, who are not responsible for the sacramental life of the church, are in no position to cause disorder through defective consecration. The ecumenical interest in deacons began soon after Vatican II. In 1964 the World Council of Churches held a consultation on "The Ministry of Deacons in the Church." This meeting resulted in the publication of two studies, *The Ministry of Deacons* (1965) and *The Deaconess* (1966).

In what has become the most influential and famous of ecumenical statements, the Faith and Order Commission, meeting in Lima, Peru, drew up *Baptism, Eucharist and Ministry* (1982), commonly called "the Lima text" or simply BEM. Section 31 deals "in a tentative way" with the functions of deacons:

> Deacons represent to the Church its calling as servant in the world. By struggling in Christ's name with the myriad needs of societies and persons, deacons exemplify the interdependence of worship and service in the Church's life. They exercise responsibility in the worship of the congregation: for example by reading the scriptures, preaching and leading the people in prayer. They help in the teaching of the congregation. They exercise a ministry of love within the community. They fulfill certain administrative tasks and may be elected to responsibilities for governance.

A commentary on the section mentions a few issues (whether there is a need for deacons, whether they need to be ordained, whether the order should be used as a stepping stone to the priesthood) and sums up:

> Today, there is a strong tendency in many churches to restore the diaconate as an ordained ministry with its own dignity and meant to be exercised for life. As the

churches move closer together there may be united in this office ministries now existing in a variety of forms and under a variety of names.[18]

Protestant churches are beginning to move in response to the BEM document. Many of them already have deacons of various kinds and names—deacons, deaconesses, diaconal ministers, home missionaries (to name the four types in Methodism)—some ordained, mostly lay. An ecumenical working party in Scotland in 1989, representing four traditions (Anglican, Methodist, Reformed, United), found this variety "not a depressing omen of the difficulty of reaching agreement, but an encouraging sign of the manifold grace of God given to the churches even in their separation." Their report, titled "Deacons for Scotland?" called for "retention of a variety of kinds of deacon in the united church in an initial period, leaving the way fully open for the church, after union, to discover what the office of deacon in the Church of God is to be."[19]

Interest in the diaconate among Methodists in New Zealand surfaced in 1984, when David S. Mullan wrote a small but important book, *Diakonia and the Moa*, in which he compared deacons to the moa, an extinct bird of that country, and urged the revival of the seemingly perished diaconate. The United Methodist Church in the United States reported that it had 1,299 diaconal ministers at the end of 1989. A UMC commission for the study of ministry has recommended replacement of the existing forms of diaconal ministry with "a permanent lay order of consecrated deacon." The commission has not yet been able, however, to define the difference between "ordination" and "consecration."[20]

In the Eastern Orthodox and Oriental churches women deacons (or deaconesses) are canonically possible, but women are currently ordained only in the

Armenian Apostolic and two other Oriental churches. According to ancient custom, the wife of a deacon may be called deaconess. There is a strong movement in Orthodox theological circles to revive the apostolic order of deaconess on the basis of many ancient prototypes and prayers.

Lutherans already have thousands of men and women deacons in Europe, and a few dozen in the United States, some of them ordained by what Anglicans consider bishops in apostolic succession. Tom Dorris, a deacon of the Metropolitan New York Synod in the Evangelical Lutheran Church in America (ELCA), works in Geneva, Switzerland, as editor of Ecumenical Press Service, a function of the World Council of Churches. Dorris travels widely, covering ecumenical news, and writes a regular column for *Diakoneo* and the Roman Catholic publication *Deacon Digest*. When he attended the Lambeth conference in 1988, he had a peculiar experience. In pre-registration forms he gave his ecclesiastical status or title as "deacon." In conference materials he was sometimes listed without title, sometimes titled "Mr.," sometimes titled "Revd."—but never titled "Deacon."[21]

The union of three Lutheran churches in the United States into the ELCA resulted in a moratorium in the ordination of deacons, but pressure for a restored diaconate continues. In 1988 two Lutherans addressed a position paper to the ELCA in which they proposed "maybe six deacons" in each church, called according to the needs of the congregation, sharing with the pastor in a collegial ministry, and giving the people support, encouragement, and guidance.[22] Meanwhile, the Evangelical Lutheran Church in Canada has published an official document that includes the recovery of the diaconate.

Although Anglican dialogue with Lutherans has dealt only tentatively with deacons, Anglican and Lutheran deacons have already made contact, and extended welcome, on their own informal level. Since 1982 the Episcopal Church has had "interim eucharistic sharing" with the ELCA. On the basis of that communion the board of trustees of NAAD decided in June 1989 to include Lutheran synods (the equivalent of dioceses) and deacons in its membership. A similar eucharistic sharing, and hence diaconal fellowship, exists in Canada.

When deacons of different traditions get together, ecumenical barriers tend to fall. The Faith and Order Commission of the National Council of Churches has held two consultations on the diaconate, on 25-27 February 1987 in Douglaston, New York, and 9-11 December 1988 in Irving, Texas, each attended by representatives from Roman Catholic and Protestant traditions. The first meeting provided an opportunity for initial sharing of theology and practice. The second meeting dealt with the practical aspects of *diakonia* and included more participation by deacons. Out of the meeting emerged a new organization, the eighteen-denomination National Diaconate Dialogue Group.

In the British Isles a similar consultation, the Scottish Ecumenical Encounter on the Diaconate (SEED), occurred on 26-30 September 1988 in Dunblane, Scotland, with thirty-two theologians, administrators, and practicing deacons (or deaconesses) from seven churches. They shared ideas, personal stories, and progress reports. The official report stated, "Throughout the encounter there was a deeply felt unity in the understanding of the diaconate as a ministry of Christ."[23] A second encounter is planned for 1991.

In many countries organizations and periodicals exist for each denomination that has deacons or diaconal ministers. In Europe such groups are prominent especially in Germany, France, Italy, and England. National types of the diaconate have evolved, which transcend denominational barriers. In Germany the Roman Catholic and Evangelical deacons tend to administer church charities, and the Evangelical social-care diaconate is slowly evolving into a ministry of word and liturgy like that of the Roman Catholic diaconate. In England the Roman Catholic and Anglican deacons tend to be liturgical and pastoral ministers in parishes, but the revival of the Anglican diaconate should result in a greater emphasis on social care. Sr. Teresa of London, observing the similarities and cross-culturization, suggests that it is more possible for deacons than for priests or pastors to work ecumenically in joint projects or with mixed recipients.[24]

The evolving fellowship of deacons is expressed through several international organizations. The largest of these is the World Federation of Diaconal Associations and Sisterhoods, known as Diakonia, founded in 1946. Until recently Diakonia was an organization of mainly protestant and women's associations, heavily Lutheran and Methodist, with some Anglican deaconesses, but its composition is beginning to change. Diakonia holds an international assembly every four years, and operates mainly for the exchange of information. Two related groups, Kaire and Koinonia-Diakonia, respond to other needs. Kaire, founded in 1978, specializes in sharing spiritual insights, through annual meetings, and includes Roman Catholics and Orthodox as well as Anglicans and Protestants. Koinonia-Diakonia specializes in theology and ecumenical fellowship, and meets irregularly. Finally, the Roman Catholics have their own world-wide group, Internationales Diakonatszentrum (IDZ), which evolved out of the original diaconate circles in 1959. Still located in Freiburg, Germany, IDZ acts as a clearing house for information.[25]

In all the ecumenical and international discussions, three themes continually appear: the theology of service and servants in the context of baptism, the spirituality of serving and being served, and identification of the needs of the world and their root causes. The participation of deacons in the ecumenical movement is a late, but fitting phenomenon. Diaconal ministry is alive and well. In churches with deacons, ordained or unordained, they serve the local assembly, they serve the poor, they serve the diocese (or equivalent) directly under the bishop (or equivalent), and they serve church unity. In churches without deacons but with other diaconal ministers, or whatever they are called, these persons also serve the assembly, the poor, and the ecumenical church.

The BEM consensus statement included the diaconate in its vision of the church. The 1987 consultation on the diaconate, sponsored by the National Council of Churches, began to bring together the servant ministers of several denominations. As they entered into dialogue, they discovered that they were caring for the same poor and representing the same servant Christ. During the next decade many churches in this country and elsewhere will specifically designate deacons and other diaconal ministers by whatever names.

ENDNOTES

1. Wilhelm Schamoni's notes (now lost) were expanded in his *Familienvater als geweihte Diakone* (Paderborn: Schoeningh, 1953), published in English as *Married Men as Ordained Deacons* (London: Burns and Oates, 1955). See Joseph Hornef and Paul Winninger, "Chronique de la restauration du diaconat (1945-1965)," in *Le diacre dans l'Église et le monde*

d'aujourd'hui, ed. Paul Winninger and Yves Congar (Paris: Les Éditions du Cerf, 1966), pp. 205-206.

2. *Council Speeches of Vatican II*, ed. Hans Küng, Yves Congar, and Daniel O'Hanlon (Glen Rock, N.J.: Paulist Press, 1964), pp. 103-104.

3. Patrick McCaslin and Michael G. Lawler, *Sacrament of Service: A Vision of the Permanent Diaconate Today* (New York and Mahwah, N.J.: Paulist Press, 1986), p. 88.

4. Thomas Ewald, "Deacon Helps Bereaved," *Deacon Digest* 7:2 (May 1990), 8-9.

5. Gordon McKibben, "The Other Side of Charles Clough," *Deacon Digest* 7:2 (May 1990), 12-13, reprinted from the *Boston Globe*.

6. Lambeth Conference 1958, *The Encyclical Letter from the Bishops together with the Resolutions and Reports* (London: SPCK, 1958), 1:50, 2:106-107. In addition to "distinctive," the committee report used the term "permanent diaconate."

7. Bishop of St Andrews [John Howe], "The Diaconate," in Lambeth Conference 1968, *Preparatory Essays* (London: SPCK, 1968), pp. 62-74.

8. Lambeth Conference 1968, *Resolutions and Reports* (London: SPCK; Greenwich, Conn.: Seabury Press, 1968), pp. 38-39. For the full text, see the Appendix.

9. Lambeth Conference 1978, *The Report of the Lambeth Conference 1978* (London: CIO, [1978]), p. 44. See also p. 81 and James B. Simpson and Edward M. Story, *Discerning God's Will: The Complete Eyewitness Report of the Eleventh Lambeth Conference* (Nashville and New York: Thomas Nelson Publishers, 1979), p. 307.

10. *ACC-3* (Report of Third Meeting: Trinidad 1976) (London: Anglican Consultative Council, 1976), p. 42.

11. *The Truth Shall Make You Free: The Lambeth Conference 1988, The Reports, Resolutions and Pastoral Letters from the*

Bishops (London: Church House Publishing, for Anglican Consultative Council, 1988), pp. 55-56.

12. *Deacons in the Ministry of the Church: A Report to the House of Bishops of the General Synod of the Church of England*, GS 802 (London: Church House Publishing, 1988).

13. *Distinctive Diaconate News* 24 (Sept. 1989), 1.

14. These publications may be ordered from 2 Tavistock Rd., London W11 1BA.

15. Reginald H. Fuller, "An Anglican Odyssey, 1987-88," *Open*, Dec. 1988, p. 3.

16. Sources on the diaconate in the Anglican communion include Bavin, pp. 43-50; Sr. Teresa, "An Anglican Perspective on the Diaconate—1988," Distinctive Diaconate Studies 29 (1988), pp. 17-19; numerous issues of *Distinctive Diaconate News*; and *Diakoneo* 10:5 (Nov. 1988), 2, 11:4 (Sept. 1989), 5.

17. *A New Zealand Prayer Book, He Karakia Mihinare o Aotearoa* (Auckland, New Zealand: William Collins Publishers Ltd, 1989), p. 897. Except for a few phrases, the ordination prayers for bishops and priests are similar to the prayer for deacons.

18. *Baptism, Eucharist and Ministry* (Geneva: WCC, 1982), p. 27. A summary of official responses from the churches, on deacons and the diaconate, appears in *Diakoneo* 10:3 (May 1988) through 12:1 (Jan. 1990).

19. *Diakoneo* 12:1 (Jan. 1990), 10.

20. *Diaconal Dialogue* (UMC), Jan.-Feb. 1990. Another recommendation called for "one ordination to the order of elder with no prior ordination as deacon."

21. Tom Dorris, "Lambeth 1988 and a Touch of Deacons," *Diakoneo* 10:5 (Nov. 1988), 3.

22. William Scar and Marianne Wilkinson, "The Renewal of the Order of the Diaconate," unpublished paper, [1988].

23. "Report of Scottish Ecumenical Encounter on the Diaconate, 26-30 September 1988" (1988), and *Distinctive Diaconate News* 23 (March 1989), 7-8.

24. *Distinctive Diaconate News* 23 (March 1989), 7.

25. For a survey of organizations, see "Report on the Fellowship (Koinonia) of the Diaconate," Distinctive Diaconate Studies 20 (1981), with updates in *Distinctive Diaconate News*, and Bavin, p. 33. For a list of periodicals, see the last section of "A Bibliography on the Diaconate, 1849-1989" (NAAD, 271 N. Main St., Providence, R. I. 02903).

6

Baptism, Ordination, and Deacons

*I*n the late twentieth century, baptism and holy orders have begun to change places in the popular view. For many members of the church, ordination and clerical status formerly represented the fullness of membership in the church, while baptism was only the first stage in the journey to orders. Now, in the writings of theologians, in the teachings of bishops, in revised liturgies, and even (if slowly) in popular opinion, a shift is beginning to take place. Returning to the traditions and belief of Scripture and the early church, we have perceived clearly that what it means to be a Christian transcends what it means to be a deacon or a presbyter or a bishop.

This change of positions has wonderful but frightening implications. The shift will take decades to implement in the practice of the church, and there is always the danger of a return to the earlier clerical model. I intend to examine some of the implications of this shift by exploring the liturgies of baptism and ordination.

Baptized to service
The great rediscovery of our age has been the meaning and practice of baptism. Despite the ancient and still-revered practice of baptizing the infants of believers, baptism is primarily for adults. It draws its meaning,

and its most appropriate occasion, from the Easter experience as it is expressed in the Great Vigil of Easter. After the people have entered the church, the deacon begins the exsultet by calling on angels, earth, and church to rejoice in the victory of Christ. The imperative *exsultet* means not only to rejoice, to feel a blissful emotion, but to leap up, repeatedly and even violently as in a wild dance. Although the action of the vigil tends to be sedentary, as Anglicans and other western Christians usually render it, I prefer to imagine the exsultet as the deacon calling a boisterous square dance. The dancers—swarms of angels, the earth and all its inhabitants (the whole Noah's Ark entourage), and Mother Church (all the people of God, living and dead)—circle round and swing their partners. In cosmic steps the dancers recall the paschal lamb and praise God for the light of Christ. A square dance is energetic but not chaotic; the dancers rarely bump into each other or step on toes. It is orderly. The figures that all perform require precise execution, and the dancers listen carefully to the caller.

This dance represents the order of creation brought to perfection through Christ. Exodus and crucifixion take place according to God's orderly plan. Here is one of the great prayers of the paschal vigil:

> O God of unchangeable power and eternal light: Look favorably on your whole Church, that wonderful and sacred mystery; by the effectual working of your providence, carry out in tranquillity the plan of salvation; let the whole world see and know that things which were cast down are being made new, and that all things are being brought to their perfection by him through whom all things were made, your Son Jesus Christ our Lord.

This prayer, which is used also as the collect at ordinations of all three orders, reminds us that the perfect order of God's church—although to our dim sight the church seldom appears perfect or orderly—is grounded in God's creation of all things.

Into this perfect order people are baptized. The baptismal process involves shedding the old life of satanic disorder and taking on the new life of God's orderly plan. This plan is outlined early in the baptismal liturgy of the Episcopal Church. After the candidates have been presented and examined, have promised to renounce Satan and turn to Christ, they swear the baptismal covenant. This covenant contains several elements essential to Christian life: *orthodoxy* (right praise of the triune God, expressed in the Apostles' Creed), *koinonia* (fellowship or shared communion), *metanoia* (change of mind or turning from evil), *kerygma* (proclamation of the gospel), *diakonia* (serving and loving Christ in others), and *righteousness* (seeking justice and peace).

The first three of these—*orthodoxy*, *koinonia*, and *metanoia*—find their proper place in the internal life of the church and its members. They are the focus of priestly or presbyteral ministry, which teaches and encourages belief, forms and builds up community, and guides the spiritual life of the people.

The fourth—*kerygma*—is both internal and external, both priestly and diaconal. The church proclaims the gospel both to its members and to the world outside. In the evangelical question the celebrant asks: "Will you proclaim by word and example the Good News of God in Christ?"

The last two—*diakonia* and *righteousness*—belong mainly (but not entirely) in the external life of the church and its members. They are the focus of diaconal ministry, which works with the helpless and tries to cure the causes of poverty and oppression. The diaconal question is central to the teaching and practice of Christ. The celebrant asks: "Will you seek and serve Christ in all persons, loving your neighbor as yourself?"

Out of this service of mercy flows a concern for justice, expressed in the last question: "Will you strive for justice and peace among all people, and respect the dignity of every human being?" The six questions will be repeated, in slightly different form, in the ordination of a deacon. In baptism, however, they refer to the ministry of all Christian people in church and world.

References to priestly and diaconal ministries appear in several other places in the baptismal liturgy. To consecrate the oil of chrism—either within the baptismal liturgy or on some other occasion—the bishop prays "that those who are sealed with it may share in the royal priesthood of Jesus Christ." After the baptism and chrismation, the people welcome the neophytes with these words:

> We receive you into the household of God. Confess the faith of Christ crucified, proclaim his resurrection, and share with us in his eternal priesthood.

The key word in both texts about priesthood is *share*. Royal or eternal priesthood is a function of the assembly. It is exercised chiefly through a shared society in which the members join in offering gifts to God: praise, intercession, confession, thanksgiving, bread and wine, incense, uplifted hands and hearts, money, food for the hungry, their own lives. All are priestly. But the emphasis is on priesthood rather than priests, on a group rather than individual persons.

The diaconal element is repeated and reinforced in the prayers for the candidates: "Teach them to love others in the power of the Spirit," and "Send them into the world in witness to your love." The element appears also in the blessing of chrism, when the bishop refers to Christ as "servant of all," and in the prayer after baptism, when the celebrant refers to these new "servants" of the

Father. Like Christ at his baptism in the Jordan, each neophyte is sealed as a servant by the Holy Spirit.

In 1987 I heard an eloquent sermon about the diaconal element in the blessing of the baptismal water. The blessing contains three images: creation, exodus, and the Lord's own baptism. When the deacon gathers up the gifts of all the people to be offered in the eucharist, this act signifies "the great cosmic liturgy of all creation, for the gifts represent the people who are to be consecrated, a sign of our becoming in Christ—the new creation won by his cross and resurrection." When the deacon proclaims the gospel and gathers up the intercessions of the church for the world, these acts strengthen us in our exodus, helping us to journey through the wilderness. When the deacon distributes the gifts of the altar, this act represents gifts "in the process of becoming through consecration, which the Spirit has blessed" and which the deacon takes into the world. The gift of water is compared to the gift of deacons in the life of the church.[1] Indeed, the water blessing (like the eucharistic blessing of bread and wine) is similar in structure and theme to the blessing or consecration of a new deacon. It begins with remembrance and thanksgiving, centers on *epiklesis*, or invocation of the Spirit, and ends with a prayer for the fruits of blessing on God's people.

There is a difference between the priesthood and servanthood we receive in baptism and the gifts of God we receive at birth. Our lives show abundant evidence of natural gifts, revealed in the diversity of our personalities and skills and professions. We are given a natural priesthood by virtue of being born, because we are made in the image of God—whether we accept this likeness or not, we still have a capacity for praise. We are also given a natural servanthood at birth: responding to the love of God who made us in his image, we tend to love and serve both God and others. The imprint of God upon us causes us to recognize the image of God in ourselves and adore the God we image. Although in society today God is not always recognized as the creator, this human capacity for praise and for service of others continues as a powerful force. The world is full of good, loving, caring persons who are not consciously Christian—indeed, who have nothing to do with a supreme being beyond a fuzzy-minded but stubborn refusal to believe and praise.

The gifts of baptism differ from natural human gifts in their focus and particularity. As royal priests we praise God not only for creation, but for the ultimate creation—the death and resurrection of Christ on the cross. The Spirit who hovered over the waters of primal creation now hovers over the waters of baptism and over the bread and wine, filling Christian lives with salvation and sanctification. Made in the image of God—as the patristic writers were fond of saying—we share in the divinity of Christ who humbled himself to share in our humanity.

As servants in Christ, we bring Christ to those we serve, we find Christ in those we serve, and at the heart of *diakonia* we identify the encounter of Christ with Christ. This is where communion meets service. The main difference between the two kinds of ministry, natural and baptismal, lies in the centrality of Christ in baptismal priesthood and servanthood. Through acts of *agape* and *diakonia* to the poor, hungry, thirsty, homeless, sick, imprisoned, oppressed, and all those in need, we discover the presence of Christ who reveals his Father and carries out his Father's work of creation and salvation.

Ordination and service

What is the meaning of ordination, a sacramental rite that stands in the shadow of the great sacrament of baptism? In the modern church, in some circles, it is fashionable to degrade the three holy orders as out-dated, of little use, and even harmful. We are right to emphasize baptism. We are wrong to treat bishops, presbyters, and deacons as mere appendages who sometimes benefit the church, mainly as functional conveniences, but who are dispensable because of the priesthood of all believers.

The preface to the ordination rites, however, claims that these three orders are "a gift from God for the nurture of his people and the proclamation of his Gospel everywhere." If nurture is shorthand for priesthood, and proclamation for servanthood, the definition may be considered sufficient. But it needs expansion.

Christ shares his *diakonia* with his church. The service of Christ thus embraces and includes the whole Christian people of God. Their membership in the eucharistic body confers on them an indelible character of *diakonia*. They are one with Christ on the cross, a cross marked forever on their forehead. They follow Christ, they love and serve the Lord, they witness to the death and resurrection of Christ. They are the *laos*, the people, the essential ministers of the church.

The *laos* are not one ministry but many. The catechism misleads some readers when it refers to the "laity" (which, in the regrettable modern sense of the word, means unordained Christians) as one "ministry" and even implies that the "laity" are a fourth order. The whole *laos* are thousands of ministries. Some ministries are symbolic, and some are functional. Some are the ordinary share of the Christian life. They occur when Christians believe in God, share with each other, turn from evil, proclaim the gospel, serve the needy, and seek justice and peace—any or all of these and more. Some ministries take place in families, and some at work. Some are specialized, and some are recognized. Most simply happen in a quiet way. Some are ordained.

The preface to the ordination rites states, in a phrase dating from the sixteenth century, that different ministries, including but not limited to the three orders, have existed in the church "from the apostles' time." Although Christ did not establish holy orders as they later came to exist, the three orders came into being within the first generation of Christians, certainly within the first century, and they were "within the Church." Because they occur within the body of Christ, as conscious and communal blessing, they are sacred. They convey meaning and have significance that other ministries of equal value do not impart.

In modern writings about holy orders, it is common to hear the terms *sacrament, sign, symbol, mystery,* and *icon.* All mean basically the same thing, and despite subtle differences I feel free to use them interchangeably. Speaking of ordained persons as sign, symbol, or mystery has a long history, going back to Ignatius of Antioch. Today the catechism says that each order "represents" a particular mode of Christ and his church, a term that emphasizes the *anamnesis* or "Christ-recalling" aspect of orders. We may also say that each order is a "sacrament" or "sign," meaning that, in the language of sacramental theology, it is "an outward and visible sign of an inward and spiritual grace," which is Christ in his church. Or that the order is a "symbol" that points to and contains a particular mode of Christ. Or that the order is a "mystery," a profundity beyond human understanding that somehow reveals the death and resurrection of Christ (the paschal mystery). Or that the order is an "icon," or image-window, through which we commune with a particular face of Christ in heaven. In all these terms Christ is the point of reference.

These terms refer to orders as states of being. In that sense they are similar to marriage, which is not a one-time sacramental event in the past (the wedding day), but a living sign of the union between Christ and his church. Similarly, order is not the "ordination" but a living sign of a manner or mode of Christian life.

What distinguishes those in holy orders from other members of the *laos* is the power to embody sign language, and the grace to embody it with God's help. They symbolize and incorporate in particular ways the numerous ministries belonging in a general way to all the people of God. This happens by a gift of the Spirit. The gift in ordination differs from the gift in baptism. In baptism the Spirit seals a neophyte as a member of the body of Christ; in ordination the Spirit bestows symbolism on one of the members. The gift of orders does not bestow a personal or inner change of character; it extends and adorns the speech of the community. It is song for the speechless, dance for the lame. The Spirit helps the ordained person to act out for the assembly the sign language the church has authorized. But the sign works differently for bishops, presbyters, and deacons.

If I were to pick a symbol for bishops, it would be the circle. Bishops encircle the church; a circle protects and preserves what is within. It keeps the shape and the body. The bishops are hands encircling the diocese and the whole church, embracing and incorporating the priesthood and the servanthood of the church. Some bishops regard their main activity as adventure, risk, and challenge—hands pushing away and out into the world—but the sign language of episcopacy points mainly to catholicity and orthodoxy. The liturgy of ordination talks about the bishop as primarily "called to guard the faith, unity, and discipline of the Church," while the ordination prayer speaks of the bishop as a shepherd and high priest who serves, pardons, offers, and oversees. The role of the bishop is not static but dynamic, for the gospel requires constant reinterpretation in the world at hand.[2]

Presbyters or priests (even to give both titles reveals the ancient confusion surrounding the order) resemble bishops on a local scale. What bishops are to the diocese, presbyters are to the local church. (The term *local church*, as currently used, can refer to both diocese and parish.) They lead the baptismal and eucharistic life in parishes, join with other presbyters in a college of elders, and share in the bishop's oversight of the diocese. Can we give them a geometric figure? It could be another circle, or circles within the bishop circle, but let us try the vertical line. As priests they symbolize hands uplifted in prayer. Especially in this post-Constantinian church in which our high priestly bishops must usually be someplace else, priests express the royal priesthood of Christ that all enter at baptism.[3]

In a tradition dating from Ignatius of Antioch, deacons are images of Christ the Servant who acts for God the Father. Although the practice of the diaconate has changed drastically through the centuries, the image has remained firm and constant. As helpers and co-workers of the bishop, deacons carry out the great work of servanthood and reveal the *diakonia* of Christ and his church, bringing into focus the great variety found in Christian ministry. In a communal dimension, deacons bring their sign of ministry into the *koinonia* of the church. Through activity, word, and example, deacons encourage, enable, enlist, engage, entice, model, lead, animate, stimulate, inspire, inform, educate, permit, organize, equip, empower, and support Christian people in service in the world, and they point to the presence of Christ in the needy. They are signs of service who uncover and explain signs of service. The human dimension of diaconal symbolism suggests that their geometric figure is the horizontal line, the sign of connection, hands reaching hands.[4]

Ordination of deacons

The best way to begin to study the diaconate is by looking at the liturgy of ordination. Although I speak here mainly of the ordination of a deacon in the Episcopal Church, the 1985 rite in the Anglican Church of Canada is almost identical, with minor differences in order and text, while the rites of other Anglican churches also agree in theology and practice. The liturgy begins with the presentation of an ordinand who has been legally "selected." In the Episcopal Church, the ordinand must declare the scriptures "to be the Word of God, and to contain all things necessary to salvation," and must swear loyalty and conformity "to the doctrine, discipline, and worship" of this church. The people consent to the ordination and promise to uphold the person in this ministry. After the singing of the ordination or other litany (all kneeling, although in some places the ordinand lies prostrate) and the collect, all sit for the readings.

The readings present some of the scriptural themes meaningful to the diaconate, especially those of proclamation and personal service. For the first reading, either Jeremiah 1:4-9 (the call of Jeremiah) or Sirach/Ecclesiasticus 39:1-8 (the scribe who studies the scriptures) may be used. Of these, Jeremiah is especially appropriate. It refers to the prophetic call, the putting of words in the prophet's mouth, which we now see as part of the diaconal office through the deacon's proclamation of the gospel. The deacon functions as primary evangelist of the congregation.

The prayer book gives three choices for the second reading: 2 Corinthians 4:1-6 (which refers to "seeing the light of the gospel of the glory of Christ" and to "ourselves as your slaves for Jesus' sake"), 1 Timothy 3:8-13 (which lists the qualifications of deacons and "the women"), and Acts 6:2-7 (choice of the Seven to wait on tables). There are two choices for the gospel: Luke 12:35-38 (slaves with "lamps lit" wait for their master to return from the wedding banquet) and Luke 22:24-27 ("I am among you as one who serves").

The preacher then delivers a homily based on the readings which covers the meaning and duties of the diaconate. Since the bishop will cover the same territory, in the formal address that follows, the preacher needs to be careful not to contradict the scriptures or the prayer book. There is a custom, whose origin and age I am unable to determine (the prayer book does not mention it), that the preacher close with a "charge," a personal address to the ordinand; some preachers omit the "charge" on the grounds that the homily should be addressed to all the people.

Talking to the ordinand is really the bishop's job. The bishop's address occurs principally in the examination, which every candidate preparing for ordination should study carefully. This is an important document for our understanding of deacons and diaconal ministry in the church. It contains two main parts, an address on the work of a deacon and a series of questions and answers. After a trinitarian prologue on baptismal discipleship— "every Christian is called to follow Jesus Christ, serving God the Father, through the power of the Holy Spirit"— the address proper consists of eight statements. The first and last statements form a bracket which opens and closes the other six. The six internal statements, each of which begins with the phrase "You are to ...," expand the meaning of the first, introductory statement:

1. *God now calls you to a special ministry of servanthood directly under your bishop.*

A multitude of relationships makes up ministry in the church, but what makes this one "special" is its link between deacon and bishop. The ancient and primary bond of deacons, deriving from ordination, is with the bishop of the diocese—first the bishop who ordained the deacon, then that bishop's successors. If a deacon moves to another diocese, and the move is canonically approved through "letters dimissory" (a certificate from the bishop which sends the deacon to the new diocese), the bond transfers to the bishop of the new diocese.

The bond of deacons with the bishop differs from that of priests, since priests work together with the bishop in a college of presbyters and take a "share in the councils of the Church." Other Christians gather around and work with the bishop, but they are free to come and go and function in all sorts of ways, which are accountable not directly to the bishop (with the exception of a few licensed ministries) but to the entire community of the baptized, and they also take part in the governance of the church. No statement, in the catechism or in the ordination liturgy, gives deacons a formal conciliar role or grants deacons a vote in church governmental bodies. The role of deacons above all involves obedience to the bishop.

Deacons are subject to the bishop because the bishop oversees *diakonia* in the church. The ancient bond between deacons and bishop—by which the deacon acted as the eyes and ears of the bishop—does not translate easily into the late twentieth century. Today priests function much as bishops did in the third century, and much of the bonding involves deacons and priests instead. Deacons and bishops, however, are seeking new expressions of the ancient bond which combine collegiality with discipline. Deacons thus help bishops to carry out their own ordination vow to "be merciful to all, show compassion to the poor and strangers, and defend those who have no helper."

2. *In the name of Jesus Christ, you are to serve all people, particularly the poor, the weak, the sick, and the lonely.*

An essential function of deacons is to serve those in need. Deacons share this ministry with all the baptized, who serve the needy in many different ways; the difference is one of focus. Deacons are to be lights of service at the center of the church. One distinctive role of deacons is to hold up mercy and justice, just as they hold up the paschal candle in the midst of all the smaller, hand-held candles of the Easter Vigil, so that the people, led and encouraged by an example of radiance, will go into a world of darkness with candles of Christ.

Former deacons aided the needy mainly within the church: the poor, old, sick, and shut-in of the parishes whom deacons visited and brought the sacrament. There is precedent for this form of ministry—the deacon of the early church who took the sacrament directly from the eucharist to Christians who could not be present, especially those in prison. But early deacons such as Laurence also found the poor in the world outside the church. In our age we regard ministry to those within the church as primarily pastoral, the work of the parish priest and certain other baptized persons; by contrast, deacons now find the *anawim* in the world at large. Poverty, weakness, sickness, and loneliness are global conditions, too broad to be limited to the membership of the church. The experience of Israel teaches us that recognition of poverty within leads to recognition of poverty without. Servant of the needy has thus become a synonym for servant of the world. The bishop's instruction "to serve all people," while including the poor, weak, sick, and lonely of the church, points through the church door to vast numbers outside.

3. *As a deacon in the Church, you are to study the Holy Scriptures, to seek nourishment from them, and to model your life upon them.*

Do we not require this study of all the baptized? Such study, nourishment, and modeling are implied in the baptismal covenant question about proclaiming the gospel "by word and example." Two questions following the bishop's address to the ordinand indicate the special importance of Scripture in the study and life of a deacon: "Will you be faithful in prayer, and in the reading and study of the Holy Scriptures?" and "Will you do your best to pattern your life [and that of your family, *or* household, *or* community] in accordance with the teachings of Christ, so that you may be a wholesome example to all people?" The bishop's address requires deacons to study the scriptures but also to live as imitators of Christ.

The personal life of deacons should include the spiritual disciplines common to all Christians: daily prayer (especially the daily office), family prayer (which includes all small groups), confession of sin, and the eucharist. The bishop's address also suggests that deacons adopt a program of regular, even daily, reading and study of Scripture and commentaries. Deacons may expand on this requirement by forming and leading groups to study the Bible.

The reason for this emphasis on the scriptures lies in the special role of the deacon as chief evangelist, the reader whose formal proclamation of the gospel encourages others to bear the Word into the world. The essence of Scripture is the *logos* or Word who is Christ. To study the Word is to feed on Christ. To model oneself on Christ is to adopt a life that is modest, simple, and humble. This is probably what the writer of 1 Timothy meant when he said that deacons "must hold fast to the mystery of the faith with a clear conscience" (1 Tim 3:9).

The mystery of the faith is the paschal mystery of Christ crucified and risen.

4. *You are to make Christ and his redemptive love known, by your word and example, to those among whom you live, and work, and worship.*

This statement bears on the symbolic nature of the diaconate. All Christians must relieve distress and seek out the causes of injustice; deacons are also symbols of the *diakonia* of Christ and his church. As we have seen, diaconal function gives life and structure to diaconal symbol. As servants of the church, deacons hold before it the whole ministry of the church as service. As symbols of Christ, deacons reveal to the people of God that they all have been baptized as servants.

As symbols of Christ, deacons occupy a special place in the *laos* as a living challenge to symbols of status and hierarchy. Although members of the clergy in canon law, they are also, in the ancient tradition of the church, members of the laity. Hippolytus said that the deacon "does not take part in the council of the clergy." The existence of deacons in the church raises profound questions about the historical development of the clergy (bishops and presbyters) into a professional estate above and separate from the vast majority of Christians. Deacons demonstrate that leadership does not have to be hierarchical.

The making known of Christ has a practical aspect— which is also controversial. As ordained persons, deacons have inherited special dress, titles, and other symbols of clerical status, yet deacons should be distinguished as servants to those among whom they live and work and whom they serve. There is evidence that men deacons (and priests) sometimes find clerical titles and collars unnecessary, because in many church circles men are assumed to be ordained, but that women deacons sometimes find them helpful as visible signs of ordination.[5] In places that deny the value of women in the church's leadership, women clerics sometimes feel compelled to adopt the signs of rank that men clerics use.

The decision about clerical dress and titles belongs to the bishop. Some bishops require street clothing as the norm for deacons, even on Sunday morning. Some bishops allow the clerical collar when a particular form of diaconal ministry requires it; some bishops require it on certain occasions, such as "when functioning as a deacon of the church." Some bishops specify "the Reverend" as a formal title for deacons, with "Deacon" for less formal address. In most American culture a clerical collar and the title "Reverend" signify someone professionally clerical, especially a hired pastor. Although clerical collars and titles are not an issue over which any Christian should make a last stand, the bishop needs to ask whether the customary styles accurately signify an ordained servant of the church.

5. *You are to interpret to the Church the needs, hopes, and concerns of the world.*

Having cared for the needy in the world, as Scripture directs all of us to do, deacons then return to the church in the role of *signifier*, or interpreter. This role has great value for the church, but first some qualification is necessary. By itself the bishop's direction to interpret the world to the church is not a license to preach. Preaching, whether by deacons or anyone else, is interpretation of the Good News as it should be lived out in the world. It is a prescription for health. Deacons interpret the world in all its messiness to the church, because as workers among the needy, they have continual access to needs, concerns, and hopes. Other workers among the needy also have access, but only deacons are directed to *interpret*.

This means that deacons must be able to see and hear and speak. Part of the training of deacons should be to teach them the many languages of the needy. This involves skills in observation, listening, diagnosis, and speaking (including musical and artistic expression). It involves knowledge about how social and political systems, institutions, and organizations work. In her speech at the Kanuga conference in 1989, Maylanne Whittall spoke of a social worker, preoccupied with Jungian psychology, who began her first interview with a client with, "How do you feel?" The street person answered, "I feel *hungry*."

Whittall suggests three guidelines for listening and diagnosis: First, we must listen where others don't—"to children, to old people, to women, to street people, to natives, to people of color, to the voice of emerging nations." Second, we must voluntarily displace ourselves into situations not normal for us. Third, we must develop "the ability, the strength, and the willingness to make ourselves inconspicuous." These guidelines help us to be attentive to the needs, concerns, and hopes of the world in which we live and work.

Deacons interpret the world to the church in several settings. They interpret when they "make known to the bishop what is necessary," as Hippolytus put it. They interpret the world when they speak out in the forums of the church, which is not the same as voting. They are expected to use their voice in conventions and on church bodies such as commissions and committees and vestries. In many parishes, deacons work with outreach committees. They interpret the world when they tell the stories and sing the songs and draw the pictures of the poor. In the liturgy, to "interpret" means to put the language of needs, concerns, and hopes into the language of bidding to prayer, as in the "prayers of the people." In the ancient language of the church at prayer, deacons are to list names and concerns of great need, so that the people can intercede through Christ to our Father in heaven.

6. *You are to assist the bishop and priests in public worship and in the ministration of God's Word and Sacraments.*

I prefer to render such instruction in these words: "In the liturgy you are to act for the assembly as proclaimer of the gospel, interpreter of the world, and waiter at the table." The point of the diaconal role in liturgy is not that a subordinate assists the presider—who can just as well do without serious help, and all too often does. The point is that a deacon, as a major performer in the assembly, plays a vital role in the complete action of the assembly by acting out messages of diaconal ministry. This performance does not take place in isolation, for the deacon works as part of a team of actors.

In the Christian liturgy, the people of God put on the masks of ancient Greek drama and bring about catharsis, sing the arias and duets and choruses of grand opera, kick up heels in a country dance, set fire and drown in water and rub oil and feed the hungry, perform for their own enjoyment and the pleasure of God. Liturgy is the closest experience of human beings to heaven on earth, and maybe it is heaven. But I speak idealistically, with a sigh for the often grim reality.

Aidan Kavanagh, in a witty little book about liturgical style, says that the deacon is "the assembly's prime minister" who must be able to perform the other ministries as well as anyone else: "singer of singers, cantor of cantors, reader of readers . . . butler in God's house, *major domo* of its banquet, master of its ceremonies."[6] There are three activities in the liturgy in which the deacon performs as angel or table waiter: proclaimer of the gospel (angel), bidder of intercessions (both angel and table waiter, delivering messages and reading lists), and table waiter at the messianic banquet (setting the table, preparing the dishes, serving the food, making sure the banqueters don't make a mess, cleaning up, telling everyone to go home). How this is done is a matter of combining ancient tradition with local custom, too complicated to describe in detail here.

One complaint about deacons, especially from bishops and priests, concerns their bumbling and bungling in the liturgy. Cooking a pot of beans for the hungry does not always translate into spreading table linens and setting bread and wine on the altar. Deacons need more help in liturgy than we have been giving them. Training should cover two areas: reading (including singing, a form of discourse that pleases God) and waiting on tables. Deacons need to learn to function in the choreographed, stylized liturgy of a cathedral as well as in an informal small setting. They need to learn to observe when help is needed—the bishop has lost his glasses!—and to spring to action at a crisis. I would put prospective deacons into a restaurant for a month or two and let them learn to reconcile the uproar in the kitchen with smooth attendance in the dining room. Another idea is to conduct a school for butlers; in the old days of high-priced oil, an English butler ran such a school in Houston, Texas. Polite manners are equally proper in a hospital ward and a soup kitchen and a prison dining hall and the Christian liturgy. I would have the trainees spend an hour a day singing the Exsultet, gospel, prayers of the people, and dismissal (especially the Easter dismissal with alleluias). Even the tone deaf and others disabled in speech or hearing can be taught to make a joyful noise. Aidan Kavanagh writes: "A deacon who cannot sing is like a reader who cannot read, a presbyter (which means elder) without age or wisdom, a bishop (which means overseer) who cannot see, a presider who cannot preside."[7] It's a harsh judgment but all too often a true picture of what goes on.

If we train deacons to act in liturgy, we must also train bishops and priests to live and work with waiters. The main problem is to teach the presider to preside and not to wait on table. Presider, stay away from the altar until your time arrives, and be a model of quiet prayer!

7. *And you are to carry out other duties assigned to you from time to time.*

This requirement concludes the sentence above, about liturgical duties. Those who assign the unspecified other duties are mainly "the bishop and priests," a collective term which implies the collegial priesthood of the diocese, and perhaps also those priests who have legitimate but limited authority over the deacon, and the deacon must carry them out. What a threat of despotic control! Any sane ordinand who takes the bishop's address seriously must be tempted to turn around and run out of church. The bishop may tell you to quit your job and get another, move to another town, move to another parish in the diocese, leave the hospital and enter prison, stop preparing babies for baptism and start collecting the dead for burial, leave the old folks' home and open a shelter for street addicts. Does this sound unreasonable? Potentially cruel? Most bishops will exercise common sense and pastoral good judgment. But if the instruction has any meaning, any force, it constitutes a binding agreement that the deacon is now at the service of the church to use for *diakonia*, wherever the bishop sees the need.

The instruction has another ominous meaning. Conventional wisdom, reflected in a doctrine such as the indelibility of orders, tends to place the internal nature of an ordained minister—what ordination does to the minister's character—ahead of the minister's being and function in the community. But an order exists for the good of the community, not of the ordained minister. Here the bishop is warning the ordinand against using the order for self: a deacon is ordained for others.

This statement is a variation of the vow of obedience, which the ordinand makes during the presentation. It is given its theological content by the last question following the bishop's address: "Will you in all things seek not your glory but the glory of the Lord Christ?" The deacon seeks God's glory by carrying out other duties assigned from time to time.

8. *At all times, your life and teaching are to show Christ's people that in serving the helpless they are serving Christ himself.*

The theological basis for this statement is Matthew 25:31-46. We are to feed the hungry, give something to drink to the thirsty, welcome the stranger, clothe the naked, care for the sick, visit those who are in prison, and care for all in need. Alongside the tabernacle in the sanctuary are temples of the Holy Spirit, the poor clamoring at the door for food, shelter, and a listening ear. Christ is present in all the needy and helpless, and he can be found especially in those at the bottom of society. The distinct role of deacons in the church is to reveal the real presence of Christ in the needy and helpless, and to carry this message to the people of God.

This is what the modern church means by deacons enabling, helping, and encouraging Christian people to serve. Deacons are to give Christian people the Christian reason to serve. Without the presence of Christ, ministry becomes institutional and impersonal, while the role of servant reverts to its secular meaning of low and mediocre status. In the liturgy the revelation of Christ in humanity occurs vividly when the deacon comes among the people and proclaims the good news of Christ to the poor in whom Christ dwells.

The liturgy continues after the examination. The ordinand kneels facing the bishop, and all others stand while a hymn invoking the Holy Spirit is sung. This is almost always *Veni Creator Spiritus* in either the old plainchant version or the waltz-like responsive version sung by bishop and people. The Pentecost sequence *Veni Sancte Spiritus* is also permitted, although at none of the ordinations I have attended in the last twenty years have I heard it sung. Both hymns are baptismal but point to the invocation of the Spirit in the ordination prayer.[8]

After a period of silence, the bishop begins the ordination prayer. It commences with an image of Christ drawn from the New Testament: "who took on himself the form of servant, and humbled himself, becoming obedient even to death on the cross" (from Phil 2:7-8). Through Christ "we know that whoever would be great must be servant of all." The bishop praises God for the diversity of ministries "and for calling this your servant to the order of deacons."

Then the bishop lays on hands and prays:

> Therefore, Father, through Jesus Christ your Son, give your Holy Spirit to N.; fill *him* with grace and power, and make *him* a deacon in your Church.

The bishop removes hands and concludes with prayer that the deacon be "modest and humble, strong and constant" and share in Christ's service.

The prayer of the Canadian church uses similar scriptural and patristic sources but arranges them differently. I find the Canadian version more coherent and graceful in style, while there is one subtle but major theological difference. In the American version the bishop prays that the Father "make" the ordinand "a deacon in your Church." *God* consecrates. But in the Canadian version the bishop prays: "Send down your Holy Spirit upon your servant N, whom we now consecrate in your name to the office and work of a deacon in the Church." The Canadian prayer expresses the reality of the Spirit acting in and through the body of Christ. Filled with God, *we* consecrate. In both the American and the Canadian prayers, only the Father is asked to give the fruits of consecration.

The people shout "Amen" (the rubric says "in a loud voice") and the deacon is vested with a stole worn over the left shoulder, which along with the dalmatic is one of the distinctive vestments of the deacon. They may be worn in several ways, according to various ancient traditions. Vestments have nothing to do with personal adornment or status; they are the formal dress of the assembly, and the assembly should have a hand in their design. They are beautiful costumes that attract the eye and capture the imagination, and emblems of dramatic parts conveying action. In "solemn" celebrations one sometimes still sees dress that suggests a performance of *The Mikado*. Modern vestments, however, convey beauty through simplicity and honesty in fabric and shape. Does your dalmatic suggest and permit the active yet graceful movement of one who delivers messages and waits on tables? Is your stole visible? What should the messengers and waiters wear at *this* wedding?

The bishop then gives the new deacon a Bible—a remnant of the medieval *porrectio instrumentorum*, or "delivery of the instruments"—and says: "Receive this Bible as the sign of your authority to proclaim God's Word and to assist in the ministration of his holy Sacraments." All too often the ceremony suggests a private gift—another study Bible added to the one the new deacon already owns. It would be more meaningful to give a lectern Bible or book of the gospels (or lectionary), which signifies proclamation in the assembly. The bishop might better say: "N., receive the gospels of Christ, whose herald you are, and proclaim the living Word." Then I would like to see the bishop give a large white hand towel to the deacon as a symbol of table waiting and footwashing.

The giving of the Bible (or book of the gospels) conveys the meaning of proclamation—deacon as angel herald. For the rest of the liturgy, however, the deacon enacts the role of table waiter; if several have been ordained, they share table duty. The bishop stays away from the altar until the new deacon finishes setting the table and preparing the food. Then the bishop comes to the table and censes the altar, if that is the custom, whereupon the deacon takes the censer and swings it toward and among the people—an angelic task—and the bishop begins the eucharistic prayer.

During the prayer the new deacon hovers nearby, helps the bishop follow the text, protects the wine from spillage and insects, and during the doxology, as the bishop lifts the bread, raises the cup of wine in a gesture of offering, while the bishop lifts the bread. The new deacon then receives communion and afterward administers the sacrament in one or both kinds. Usually the bishop takes the bread and the deacon the wine, but if there are several new deacons they may take both. After communion the bishop leaves the remaining sacrament on the altar and the deacon performs the ablutions. The rubrics suggest that the deacon remove the vessels, consume the remaining bread and wine, and clean the vessels "in some convenient place" (either credence table or sacristy). The deacon gives the dismissal, which should actually send people out of the church.

After the liturgy, an ancient addition to the liturgy may take place. The deacon may carry the sacrament, preferably both bread and wine, "to those communicants who, because of sickness or other grave cause, could not be present at the ordination." This obviously refers not to *nominal* Christians but to *faithful* communicants who would have been there if they could. I suggest that the new deacon publicly enlist lay eucharistic ministers to help in this extension of the body of Christ.

I have gone into detail about the ordination and eucharist in which the deacon first functions because they inaugurate the meaning of the deacon's ministry. In every Sunday eucharist, in baptisms, and in the great liturgies of Holy Week and the paschal feast, the people learn through the drama of the liturgy that to be a Christian means to be a servant of the Lord and a servant of the poor. Their vow to uphold the deacon in ministry includes upholding the deacon in liturgical performance. The people are not passive listeners at a lecture on ethics, but part of the great drama of Christ the Servant on the cross. What they enact, they are. The old axiom *lex orandi, lex credendi* means: the law of prayer [is] the law of belief. Worship constitutes and forms belief. Liturgy forms the people of God in the life of Father, Son, and Holy Spirit.

Here is another axiom. Those who act in liturgy (especially those whom the church officially appoints) must also act in the work of service in the world. As Gail Ramshaw writes, "Simply said, here is the liturgical logic: that the weekly ritual of assembling around Christ in prayer for the world will form in Christian people the mind of praise and the habit of service."[9] When one who works with the poor also proclaims the good news, calls on the people for prayers of compassion, and waits on the table, and the people recognize the connection between deacon's ministry without and deacon's ministry within, liturgy forms the people of God in a life of Christian service.

ENDNOTES

1. Richard F. Grein, "Homily of Richard of Kansas," *Diakoneo* 9:3 (Nov. 1987), 3-4.

2. For a summary of Anglican thought on bishops, see Richard A. Norris, "Episcopacy," in *The Study of Anglicanism*, ed. Stephen Sykes and John Booty (London: SPCK; Philadelphia: Fortress Press, 1988), pp. 296-309.

3. For a summary of Anglican thought on priests, see John B. Webster, "Ministry and Priesthood," in ibid., pp. 285-290.

4. For extended definitions of the diaconate, see *Deacons in the Ministry of the Church*, pp. 77-99; Anglican Church of Canada, Committee on Ministry, *A Plan to Restore the Diaconate in the Anglican Church of Canada* (Toronto:Anglican Church of Canada, 1989), pp. 4-8; and Sr. Teresa, CSA, "An Anglican Perspective on the Diaconate," Distinctive Diaconate Study 29 (1988).

5. *Distinctive Diaconate News* 24 (Sept. 1989), 6.

6. Aidan Kavanagh, *Elements of Rite: A Handbook of Liturgical Style* (New York: Pueblo Publishing Co., 1982), p. 76.

7. Ibid., p. 32.

8. Hymns 502 or 504, 503, and 226 in *The Hymnal 1982*.

9. Gail Ramshaw, "Formation in Prayer and Worship: Living the Eucharistic Prayer," in *The Baptismal Mystery and the Catechumenate*, ed. Michael W. Merriman (New York: Church Hymnal Corp., 1990), p. 73.

7

The Finding, Nurture, and Care of Deacons

G ood deacons are found, not made, but once found they must be cultivated. Touch them, lay hands on them with prayer. Tend them. Like any new plant in the garden, they need fertilizer and water, protection from bugs and disease, potting, propping, and pruning, space to grow, and most of all words of encouragement. With these as our general principles, this chapter will deal with the particulars: the three main types of deacons, diaconate programs in dioceses, and the four components of a program. Let us look at the realities, the specifics, and the rules.

Types of deacons

Deacons who work mainly on a parish staff—although much of their work may be outside the church—are commonly known as parish-based deacons. In the United States they are usually (but not always) non-salaried and part time; in England, about one-half of these deacons are salaried. They serve under the over-sight of the bishop exercised through the rector. This is the most common type of deacon.

Deacons who work mainly on the diocesan staff are commonly known as diocese-based deacons. Often (but not always) salaried and often full time, they serve under the immediate oversight of the bishop or of someone appointed by the bishop. But these deacons are still based in a parish, or sometimes the cathedral, where they perform in the liturgy. Diocese-based deacons help to strengthen the relationship between the bishop and the diocese. They symbolize the servanthood of the church to the diocesan family, providing diaconal ministries of administration or oversight. In some dioceses the bishop appoints a diocese-based deacon (or parish-based deacon) as archdeacon, with duties of oversight among the community of deacons.

Deacons who work for the most part outside the church are sometimes known as professional (or special) deacons, who share many similarities with both parish-based and diocese-based deacons. They too are assigned to a parish as their liturgical base, where they usually work without salary and part time, but their external occupation is usually professional and salaried, such as employment at state or private institutions, where they minister in hospitals, prisons, social agencies, and similar establishments. In this role they can help congregations relate more effectively to the government or public sector. This professional category also includes deacons who are members of religious orders; despite potential conflict between a vow of obedience to a bishop and a religious superior, several orders have called members to the diaconate.

Diaconate programs

Diaconate programs have spread and developed in the Episcopal Church since the mid-1970s, and it is now generally recognized that six conditions must exist for a program to be healthy and beneficial.

First, the diocese should already have a program of enabling the ministry of all its people. By whatever name this program is called—such as total or mutual ministry—it must avoid the assumption that ministry is reserved for the clergy. The diocese must promote ministry to the poor and needy in particular; to have deacons, you must first have diaconal ministry.

Second, the diocese should have a clear theology of the diaconate, grounded in scriptural and patristic concepts of *diakonia,* and coherent with the theology expressed in the catechism and ordination rite. The bishop should understand the theology and teach it to both priests and people, since it is especially important that the priests support the bishop in plans for a diaconate program.

Third, the bishop and the diocese should be committed to the diaconate program in terms of: *people* (directing the program should be the major responsibility of one person or the substantial responsibility of several), *time* (the program should continue for at least several years), and *money.* How this works out depends on the diocese's size, geography, demographics, and financial resources. Small or poor dioceses are just as able to commit people, time, and money as large or rich ones. They just don't commit them in the same way or in the same quantities.

Fourth, the program should unite deacons and other Christians in close cooperation. Deacons support others in their vocations in the wider community. Deacons and other persons may be involved in planning and administering the program: many a program has succeeded mainly because a key lay person was brought in at the beginning and threw some support behind it. And deacons-to-be, while they are still in formation, should have the opportunity to practice theological reflection with other Christians.

Fifth, a separate diaconate committee of the commission on ministry should be formed for policy, recommendations, and monitoring of the program, while a committee or similar body is needed to oversee the program. Strictly speaking, it need not be connected with the commission on ministry, but since the latter is meant to provide "for the guidance and pastoral care of Clergy and Lay Persons who are in stipendiary and non-stipendiary positions accountable to the Bishop" (canon III.2.2[c]), such a connection is desirable.

Sixth, the program should draw on the ecumenical and secular resources of the area or region, going well beyond its own denomination. This simply recognizes two realities: the pluralism of modern society, especially of Anglicanism, and the universality of the gospel. The experience of many dioceses is that deacons (and others) gain a great benefit from formation and continued contact with Christians and others outside their denominational circle.

A diaconate program should have four components: recruitment and selection, formation, deployment, and supervision and support. The diaconate committee does not displace the canonical roles of the bishop, standing committee, and commission on ministry in the ordination process, but assists them. As a program matures, wherever possible a deacon should be named director or coordinator. Bishops who appoint archdeacons (who are themselves deacons) for this purpose are restoring one of the earliest practices of the church. The director works with the bishop and the commission on ministry to administer the program, and is accountable to the bishop. In particular, the director helps the bishop in recruitment, deployment, and supervision and support. The director may chair the diaconate committee.

Ideally the director of training should be a separate person, with experience in adult education. Increasingly, deacons and other baptized persons are taking on this role.

The program should be designed to take account of the size and character of the diocese. What works for a large metropolitan diocese may not work for a small rural diocese, and vice versa. In particular, small dioceses tend to have limited amounts of people and money. Sometimes small dioceses are more committed to the renewal of the diaconate than large ones.

Finally, the program should include provision for review and evaluation of its deacons' progress and formation.

Recruitment and selection

> All Bishops of Dioceses and other Clergy shall make provisions to identify fit persons for Holy Orders and encourage them to present themselves for postulancy. [canon III.4.1]

Enacted by General Convention in 1988 to cover both presbyters and deacons, this canon appears to require a sharp change in the practice of the church. Actually, priests have been identifying and putting forward "fit persons" for centuries—although ordinary Christians usually contributed little to the process. What is new is the change in emphasis. Formerly deacons were thought of as receiving an inner call from the Holy Spirit, and the church responded with assent and validation; now they receive an outward call from the church, and those who are inwardly disposed to the ministry of deacon are moved to accept. The old canons on ministry reflected a theology of personal inspiration to vocation, while the new see the bestowal of holy orders as a function of the body of Christ. God the Holy Spirit calls through the church. This theology, although scriptural and ancient, had almost vanished before the reforms of recent decades. In ordination rites today, the bishop asks: Are you "truly called by God and his Church?" in contrast to the older version: Are you "inwardly moved by the Holy Ghost?"

The importance of an inner call has not vanished, however; it is revealed in a life of service, in good reputation, in willingness to act as deacon. But the outward call claims first place; it also comes from God, but it is spoken within the church. No longer are we to wait for applicants who have been inwardly moved before we test and screen and validate them; instead we are to recruit those with the gift of diaconal ministry, select those who are qualified, and call them.

How this is supposed to work is not as clear as the principle. Cast lots? Elect? Some subtle mechanism? In February 1989 Bishop George Harris of Alaska and his assistant, Andrew Fairfield, visited Kivalina, an Eskimo village on the Arctic coast, which then had three local priests and a local deacon. They gave all church members over the age of sixteen a slip of paper and asked them to write the names of those they thought should serve as the next generation of priests and deacons. The slips were gathered and offered to God at the altar. Then the bishop and priest spent a month thinking and praying about the nominees, made choices, and informed those who had been chosen. They were asked to think and pray for a month and give their answer. If they said no, no one knew and no one was embarrassed. If they said yes, they started on the road to ordination.[1]

Would this selection process work in a less isolated and more pluralistic community? Maybe—with serious preparation of the community and with a little tinkering with the machinery. Selection of deacons should occur as part of a larger process whereby the church discerns the needs of the church's own life and of the world and the gifts of the church's people. Dioceses and parishes first help all people to discover and evaluate their own ministries. When this has been done, each local church, each parish, can identify and raise up priests, deacons, and various other priestly and diaconal ministries from its own membership.

Early in the process the community decides to distinguish between those best suited to priesthood and those suited to the diaconate. Priesthood requires pastoral or presbyteral skills, including community formation, organization, and administration, as well as skill in preaching and leading worship. The diaconate requires skills in helping people, mediation, and advocacy. Those most suited to the diaconate must already be strongly "diaconal."

The initial stage of recruitment and selection is a delicate period in which the congregation plays a crucial role. It must also be willing to involve itself in the preparation of persons for the diaconate. The parish that has never seen a deacon must find out more about them by inviting deacons to speak and perform in the liturgy. Obviously the parish where deacons are to officiate must clearly want them, as must the priest. After that, the congregation must be carefully prepared, potential deacons screened, and a thoughtful consensus reached. Finally, the potential deacons may or may not have considered the diaconate before their selection. They have the right to accept or to refuse this call. Similar principles apply to the selection of diocese-based and professional deacons.

In the Alaskan selection described above, the bishop's request for names on slips of paper took place well before the canonical steps began. In canon law it takes place later, after a potential applicant meets with the priest, but we will be wise not to single out particular persons until God has had a chance to act within the assembly. In Scripture and the early church, the assembly chose and the person responded. However it takes place, the process requires the utmost care and sensitivity for the persons involved and for the health of the community.

In small dioceses like Western Kansas, the bishop chooses the deacons. There is ancient precedent—and sometimes modern justification—for such a method, which ought to be used discreetly and only in dioceses where the bishop knows all the people. Even then, the bishop will be wise to consult the congregation.

The personal qualifications of a potential deacon are drawn from Acts 6:3 and 1 Timothy 3:8-13. Men and women chosen for the diaconate should be "of good standing, full of the Spirit and of wisdom." They should be admired and respected, with a stable life rooted in family, community, and church. They should possess evident gifts of God, as well as be physically, emotionally, and spiritually mature. They should have intellectual ability and competence, although lack of formal academic training should not be a barrier and their primary language need not be English. Each deacon needs practical gifts in a few diaconal areas, whether it is listening to old ladies or organizing a meal for one hundred people.

In evaluating these qualifications, the congregation and bishop should ask several questions. If the person is married, does the husband or wife approve and support ordination to the diaconate? What is the person's work history? How long has the person performed *diakonia*? Has the person functioned only within the church, or gone outside it in works of social care? How is the ministry rated by those whom the person serves? Is the person willing to remain a deacon for life?

The answers to these questions, along with personal and community knowledge, will prove of far greater value than the battery of tests and sophisticated interviews we have developed in the last two decades. One of the sharpest complaints about the ordination process for both deacons and presbyters is that it consists of a seemingly endless series of evaluations by persons and groups, constantly changing in membership, all of whom can say no and none of whom can say yes. The finding of deacons, as practiced in most dioceses, is a cumbersome and drawn-out process. We require a prospective deacon to pass numerous inspections—by commissions and committees, educators, doctors, and psychologists. Most of these faceless persons and groups are far removed from the community in which the deacon will officiate. It is almost as clumsy these days to find a deacon as to elect and ordain a bishop, and it takes a lot longer. The system rewards evasion and smooth talk, punishes creative folly, and all too often produces ordinands who are cynical and bland.

The present canonical process also requires five interviews or examinations and five forms to fill out, before the bishop admits a postulant. There are five more pieces of paper and at least one interview before candidacy, and seven forms and possibly four interviews or examinations (not counting academic ones) before ordination. All this involves pointless duplication: three certificates from the person's priest and vestry and two visits each to medical and psychological examiners. Meanwhile, the person must go through two major steps: postulancy, a period of probation and early preparation for ordination, lasting at least six months, and candidacy, a period of final preparation, lasting one year (although it may be shortened to six months).

This procedure ought to be greatly simplified and shortened. We can trust God to act through the gathered people, but if we do not trust the people, we can at least design a better hurdle. Acts 6 suggests a process begun and completed entirely within a community of believers, and quickly. The local Christian people select or elect— the precise method depends on circumstances—from among those with good qualifications. From such persons each congregation chooses one or two deacons (maybe more, if the congregation is large). The bishop (advised by the commission on ministry) and the standing committee agree. The decision to ordain can be made near the beginning of the process, soon after the congregation has chosen. The church should say yes or no at the beginning and stick with it, with interviews and paperwork held to the minimum. The period before postulancy can be short and (barring an unforeseen reversal) produce approval of ordination; postulancy (but why postulancy?) and candidacy should be used solely to help ready the person for ordination. If the rules do not allow early decision, let us rewrite the rules!

Alaska and several other dioceses use the provision for local deacons (and priests) "in communities which are small, isolated, remote, or distinct in respect of ethnic composition, language, or culture" (III.9). Recognized as leaders in the congregation and "firmly rooted in the community," local deacons are modeled on the deacons of the New Testament and early church. With further simplification of the canonical steps, this provision could be used for all the deacons of the Episcopal Church.

Deacons ordained under both canon 6 (normal deacons) and canon 9 (local deacons) are specifically called to the diaconate. They present the standing committee with a signed statement that they do not intend to apply for ordination to the priesthood. The canons consider these deacons permanent, but allow for a later call to the priesthood. To become priests, such deacons must be recruited and selected for that order, undergo priestly education (often attending residential seminary), and fulfill the requirements of canon 7, except for ordination to the diaconate.

One danger of the outward call, as voiced by a local community, is that it may encourage a purely local ministry. A deacon is ordained to serve more than the place where the ordination occurs. A deacon is ordained to serve the Lord, the church, and the world, wherever he or she is called and authorized now and in the future. This is true even of "local" deacons who serve under canonical restrictions to place.

Formation and Training

Getting ready for ordination is only a small part of a lifelong process. Formation of diaconal character begins in infancy, includes the grace of Christ the Servant received in baptism, and continues for life. Canon law uses the term *preparation* to refer to the course of study and training for ordination. Preparation for ordination involves a specific application of diaconal formation, in which a person learns the rudiments of how to function in the symbolic role of deacon. The terms *formation* and *training* are widely used for this time of preparation.

Preparation has three parts: *academic* study, *practical* training or experience, and *spiritual* development or discipline. The type of formation in each area depends on individual background and circumstances, as well as on the church's need for a particular ministry. Fit the preparation to the candidates. A person may already have theological education, experience in diaconal ministry, and spiritual discipline; even so, some formation is essential. Most persons will need to review the church's basic teaching (concentrating on Scripture), sharpen diaconal skills, and participate in diaconal community. The primary focus should be on using Scripture to reflect on life. Before ordination they need to learn about service and servants in the scriptures and the church, as well as how to perform in the liturgy. If they are to work for mercy and justice, they need to learn about ethics. They need to learn collegiality—how to work with others as enhancers of ministry, how to carry out the orders of the bishop, and how to speak for others. Most of all, they need to pray.

Not everyone should prepare in the same way. The diaconate is a polychrome ministry with a great diversity of types, and ideally programs will help people prepare in ways suitable to each individual and each proposed ministry. The oldest type of diaconate training in the Episcopal Church is reading for orders: private study under the direction of one or more tutors. Its continued use in some places is cause for lament, because solitary study does a poor job of preparing a person for communal ministry. Even in remote settings, or in dioceses with no other candidates, other parishioners can be included. Many dioceses find it desirable to train deacons in small groups, where people may reflect on and share what they have read. They learn to think theologically about their ministries of social care, and to deal emotionally and spiritually with pain, disappointment, and failure. It would be helpful for such groups to include spouses.

Three main types of training have emerged in the Episcopal Church: the diocesan school for deacons, the diocesan school of theology or ministry, or some combination of the two.

The diocesan school for deacons focuses on training for the diaconate, and is highly successful at building a community of deacons; it provides role models, creates diaconal identity, and involves the sharing of stories. Until recently it has tended to be organized along seminary lines; one school has state certification and even awards degrees (e.g., bachelor of the diaconate). The tendency today, however, is to downplay academic erudition (except for the study of Scripture) and to emphasize practical training and spiritual formation. The Rhode Island School for Deacons, which meets one weekend a month, teaches Bible, church history, theology, and liturgics, and requires students to write papers and take exams, but it also devotes one semester a year to practical training, with each student doing field work in hospitals, parishes, or a specially chosen field. The school stresses the relationships of deacons to individuals and within groups (as member and as leader) and spirituality (also individual and group). In a few places the diocesan school trains deacons for several surrounding areas. The California School for Deacons, for example, includes students from the dioceses of California, El Camino Real, San Joaquin, and Northern California. Despite the name of the school, students do not have to be in the canonical track for the diaconate, and the emphasis in recent years has shifted to training for diaconal ministry in general.

The diocesan school of theology or ministry prepares an assortment of persons: those not seeking ordination at all, candidates for the diaconate, and in some dioceses, candidates for the priesthood. There are several long-standing schools of this type, including the Mercer School in Long Island, the Whitaker School of Theology in Michigan, and the Anglican School of Theology in Dallas. In some dioceses this type of school makes use of programs like the four-year curriculum "Education for Ministry" (EFM) for the academic portion. In many places EFM *is* the school for ministry, with groups meeting once a week during the academic year in many scattered locations. Groups meet once a week during the academic year for four years. Written materials cover the history of the people of God from the sources of the Pentateuch to the present day. In one diocese, the formation program combines EFM with monthly seminars attended by the prospective deacons, clinical pastoral education in a hospital, a year of social internship, and a year of parish internship.

Sometimes a school for deacons decides to branch out into lay ministry, or vice versa, which creates two or more tracks within the school. For example, someone may study for two or three years in the diocesan school for ministry and then continue with other candidates for the diaconate. In Central Florida the two-year School of Diaconal Training is a separate school within the diocesan Institute for Christian Studies. In the first year of the diaconal school, students study the history, theology, and ministry of the diaconate; in the second year they reflect in groups. Practical training takes place both years. Formation in Northern Indiana takes place in three tracks: three-year school for all the baptized, one-year deacon school, and continuing education. The deacon track concentrates on the deacon in Bible, church, world, liturgy, and pulpit.

As dioceses move away from the seminary model, they often attempt creative and unusual methods of formation. The Fort Worth formation program—at this writing in its second year—is based on the examination of a deacon in the ordination rite. It attempts an experiential model rather than one based on the more customary classroom method. The program is designed on the premise that a majority of baptized but unordained persons (including those preparing to become deacons) are "sensing" types, to use Myers-Briggs terminology, whereas a majority of priests are "intuitive" types. Thus training heavily emphasizes learning through interpretation of experience, leading to action and prayer. Formation consists of seven phases, each with three or four steps. Each phase, building on the previous one, takes three to six months to complete (a total of 21 to 42 months). At the end of each phase students present a paper and tell their story to the diaconate committee.[2]

A diocese starting or reforming its diaconate program should begin with the needs and expectations of its deacons; canon law can be adapted to human needs. The Episcopal Church's canonical requirements for academic, practical, and spiritual preparation include Scripture, church history, theology, ethics, studies in contemporary society (including ethnic and minority studies), liturgy, and the theory and practice of ministry. Nevertheless, dioceses should avoid the seminary model as much as possible, since the ministry of deacons is entirely different from that of priests. Traditional academic methods such as lectures may sometimes be used with good effect, but other forms of methodology, such as those employed on the retreats, weekend seminars, and experiential courses widely used in adult education, may also be explored.

The core of academic formation is Scripture. All Christians with even modest intellectual capacity can acquire a comprehensive knowledge of the Bible and use this knowledge to reflect theologically about problems in the church and the world. They can learn the church's basic teaching in Scripture, doctrine, liturgy, history, and ethics, but deacons need two special subjects, too. First, they need to study the history of the diaconate, including its biblical and primitive roots and its contemporary commitment to the corporal and spiritual works of mercy and to the quest for justice. Second, they need training in the role of the deacon in the liturgy, to perform with skill and grace.

Practical training usually refers to supervised practice in the particular ministry of social care proposed for the deacon, including CPE in a hospital or prison, training in social work, or training in catechetical techniques. No matter how much previous experience they have, deacons must also learn how to work as part of a team, how to work with volunteers, and how to strengthen others in their vocation in the world. In many dioceses, practical training has come to occupy a place at least equal to, and sometimes higher than, academic study.

Spiritual development or discipline is not covered in the canons, but it is an integral part of Christian life and must not be neglected. Traditional methods include regular worship, the daily office, other daily prayer and Scripture reading, retreats, and the use of a spiritual director or confessor. Prayer should take place privately and in community, especially in families. Regular self-examination and confession of sin is important, as is regular participation in support groups including spouses, families, parishioners, and deacons, and in the total life of the community. Some dioceses provide a course in spirituality for deacons and others training in ministry. Although deacons are typically formed in small groups, spiritual formation that initiates them into an exclusive club should be avoided, since the spiritual life of deacons is part of the life of the whole Spirit-filled church.

An especially appealing form of spiritual formation takes place in the diocese of Hawaii. The diocese puts on a six-month course in spiritual development, to discern any form of ministry. All those headed for ordination must take the course before they begin formal training.

The length of preparation for ordination to the diaconate normally ranges from two to four years. An overly extended period deprives parishes and dioceses of the deacons they have selected, while deacons requiring more than four years to complete formation should probably be dropped from the program. If the person is already diaconal, lengthy preparation is unnecessary. The seven men of Acts 6 were already formed in the way of Christ, although the apostles laid hands on them with what some today might call undue haste! Similarly, in the modern church preparation for ordination can be short and concentrated. Since theological knowledge is no longer the privilege and sole possession of bishops and presbyters, many "ordinary" Christians are thoroughly familiar with the Bible, discuss theology and ethics in depth, and possess skills for ministry. If we choose diaconal Christians, they will already have many skills needed for the diaconate.

Examinations and evaluations frequently terrify candidates. The canons state that for *academic* study the candidate must "pass an examination, the form and content of which shall be determined by the Bishop and the Commission." The exam may be written or oral or both; it may consist of essays, true or false questions, or both. Examiners should remember, however, that candidates for the diaconate are not students in graduate school. Usually they have been long out of high school or college and have forgotten how to take exams.

For *practical* training no exam is required. Those in charge submit to the commission on ministry a record of the training and a written evaluation of the candidate's proficiency. For *spiritual* discipline the only requirement is for the candidate to communicate with the bishop personally or by letter, four times a year, in the Ember Weeks, reflecting on academic experience and personal and spiritual development.

Deacons can be ordained either in the parish church that originally selected them or in a diocesan gathering. The eucharist at diocesan convention is sometimes used for this purpose. We make too much fuss over ordination; many outshine baptisms and even weddings. The main problem is that all ordinations, to all three orders, appear to celebrate an elevation in status. The bishop may decide instead to use the ordination liturgy to celebrate the ministries of all the people, of whom one or a few happen to be deacons.[3]

Finally, I wish to set forth a serious statement of priorities. In the process of ordaining a deacon, recruitment and selection are far more important than preparation. If we select "diaconal people," the diaconate will likely follow. For deacons the most important part of their formation takes place after ordination, is lifelong, and takes account of changing circumstances in the life and ministry of the deacons.

Every bishop should require the deacons of the diocese to follow a plan for continuing education, and many dioceses are shifting the weight of formation to the post-ordination period. In Pittsburgh the formation program, called ACTS (Academy for Christian Thinking and Service), is divided into two years of academic, practical, and spiritual formation and, after ordination, two years of continuing education (one of them as a deacon intern). In Rio Grande, where those selected must already be practicing ministry, preparation takes only one year, and continuing education is unlimited. The easiest way to fulfill the requirement is to gather the deacons for a week every summer with the bishop and spend it in community, teaching, worship, and relaxation.

Deployment of deacons

The sending of deacons into fields of ministry is part of the mission of the church, the bishop's ancient and vital function of assigning deacons to work in the church and the world. The bishop normally assigns deacons to the parish which originally chose them. or to the cathedral or some other parish, where the priest and vestry must request, or consent to, the assignment. There they function under the surrogate leadership and authority of the priest (and in some places, the vestry). It is important to understand, however, that deacons in parishes are not "curates" or "assistants" selected at the priest's discretion. They are "deacons," often called by the parish out of its membership, and appointed by the bishop as the bishop's deputies and emissaries. Chapter 8 examines in greater depth the enormous range of ministries these deacons undertake.

In some dioceses the bishop normally appoints deacons to another parish than the one from which they came, or rotates deacons every few years. This practice is usually feasible only in compact or metropolitan dioceses, where it does not cause hardship for the deacons and their families. In every diocese, however, deacons must be ready and able to respond to the bishop's call to function anywhere in the diocese. Flexibility and adaptability—the characteristics of Stephen and Philip—sometimes call for change of place or ministry or both. Some bishops leave deacons in the same place and same ministry until old age or death, while others move them often, but such policies do not always take account of the needs of the person or of the community. The consent of the rector and vestry should be a continuing requirement, periodically renewed. But the deacon's personality, family, job, talents, and changing circumstances are equally important. The deacon too has a right to request or consent to assignment, including a change.

Most parish-based deacons work for the church part time without cash stipend, housing, or housing allowance, although some are paid a stipend. The diocese or the parish may, at its discretion, cover expenses such as a car allowance and funds for continuing education, and may also provide for deacons to participate in the group life insurance and medical insurance programs of the diocese.

Diocesan and professional deacons are usually assigned to the cathedral or to the parish from which they were originally called. Diocesan deacons function in a variety of jobs: administrators, archdeacons, chancellors, treasurers, secretaries, business managers, other office workers, directors of religious education, journalists, and holders of other professional positions. They may also be institutional workers such as chaplains, social workers, and agency directors. Professional deacons perform in many of the same jobs, but outside the church.

The ancient practice of bishops naming a deacon as archdeacon has been revived in at least four dioceses. The archdeacon is primarily to direct and support the deacons of the diocese. Ordained in Idaho in 1984, Sarah Tracy came into Northern Indiana with her husband Paul, a priest, and set out to catch the ear of her bishop, William Sheridan, who sometimes responded to her daring suggestions with "Oh, Sarah!" Tracy advises deacons in similar situations, "Don't give up. The only person who likes change is a wet baby." After her new bishop, Francis Gray, named her archdeacon in 1989, she received a few letters addressed affectionately to "the Venomous"—a pun on the customary title of an archdeacon, "the Venerable." Tracy also functions as education consultant of the diocese and as director of the diocesan School for Faith and Ministry. By emphasizing formation as a spiritual journey, she has helped transform her diocese into a model of shared ministry.

Deacons may also have jobs with many of the duties, but not the title, of archdeacon. Carol Snell formerly administered the Central Pennsylvania diocesan office, where she coordinated conventions and conferences, assisted with deployment, and provided assistance and materials to parishes. In Central Florida, Linda Bronsted directs the two-year School of Diaconal Training. Kay Wood of Colorado directs the diocesan Institute of Theological Studies and leads the diocesan diaconate program, while Jim Thompson of Oregon was formerly the bishop's executive assistant and director of vocations.

Important diocesan positions are held by many deacons, such as Barbara Ranmaraine of Minnesota, who is blind and coordinates the diocesan Ministry of Persons with Handicaps as well as the diocesan Department of Social Ministries, and Carmen Anderson of Kansas, who chairs the diocesan Task Force on Ministry of the Baptized to enhance the shared ministry of all baptized people. In several dioceses a deacon works as director of the diocesan camp or conference center, while it is increasingly common for deacons to provide assistance to the church, with a strong element of outreach, on the level of a parish, deanery, region, or ecumenical group. Three Rhode Island deacons function in this way: Ted Hallenbeck, a professional fund-raising consultant and an authority on personal ministry planning, consults in parishes during interims to help them in goal setting, priorities, and the search process. Robert Johnson is executive director of Providence In-Town Churches Association, and Edmund Mayo consults with parishes for interim planning and search.

Ordination to the diaconate permanently confers the grace to symbolize the church's ministry of service, but assignments are never permanent. Deacons who move to another community or diocese, or who cease to function in a parish or diocese, lose the right to function as deacon and to symbolize *diakonia*, unless they receive a new assignment. Deacons who arrive in a new parish may not function as deacon until assignment by the bishop, with the consent of the priest and vestry.

Once assigned, deacons function in three primary areas: pastoral care among the church's own people, social care in society at large, and liturgy. Christ's washing of his disciples' feet in John 13:1-15 symbolizes all three areas. In the parish they help by visiting the sick, infirm, and newcomers, leading music, teaching children or adults (especially in the preparation of catechumens), organizing retreats and other spiritual activities, training readers and acolytes, leading prayer and discussion groups, editing and writing for newspapers and newsletters, working in parish or diocesan administration. These deacons support the baptized in their ministries in the wider community.

In the area of social outreach, deacons lead and encourage others in works of mercy and justice outside the church with prisoners, the old, the sick, the poor, the homeless, the handicapped, abused women, alcoholics, addicts, and their families, and numerous others in need. In a recent expansion of diaconal ministry, they also discern this calling in others and encourage them in their vocation. Deacons are involved in politics, business, culture, and local community development. Some social ministries unfold as part of the professional occupation of deacons, and not only with the obvious examples of deacon doctors, nurses, lawyers, and teachers. The church may also decide to put some deacons on salary to perform a vital social ministry.

In the liturgy, deacons visibly enact the *diakonia* of Christ and his church in the eucharist. Representing both angelic messenger and ordinary table waiter, deacons proclaim the gospel, bid the prayers of the people, wait on the table, administer the cup, dismiss the people, give directions, and keep order. On the three days of the paschal feast (Maundy Thursday night, Good Friday, and the Easter Vigil), deacons play a major role in enacting the mystery of Christ's death and resurrection. Deacons also take the eucharistic bread and wine to the sick and infirm, direct the lay eucharistic ministers, and assist in Christian initiation, marriage, and burial. In all liturgies it is proper for two or three deacons to attend the bishop and share functions, and two deacons are appropriate in the parish liturgy.[4]

In a few limited situations, deacons are permitted to preside. This permission is to be considered an aberration, since they symbolize diaconal ministry best when they act as messengers and attendants. Deacons may preside, however, at a communion service (this term is preferable to "deacon's mass") or liturgy including distribution of the reserved sacrament to a congregation. This is a liturgy that should be used only when no priest is available and the permission of the bishop has been received either in advance or soon after (in an emergency). Both deacons and lay persons may also anoint the sick when necessary, using oil previously blessed by a bishop or priest; they may hear confessions of sin, but they may not pronounce absolution. In both sacramental rites the normal officiant is a bishop or priest.

Another area of confusion with the priestly role is preaching. Only bishops and priests are ordained specifically to preach. At ordination the bishop directs a candidate for priest to preach, but gives no such direction to a candidate for deacon who is told instead "to interpret." The bishop may license baptized persons to preach liturgical homilies, after study and practice, but there is no canonical provision for licensing deacons. Some bishops assume that deacons automatically have the ability or right to preach as an extension of the bishop's ministry. Those who are talented preachers may be given appropriate opportunities to exercise this gift.

Sometimes deacons ignore or break the ordination mandate to serve the helpless. Deployment refers not only to parish assignment, but includes works of mercy and justice in the world. Failure to perform these good works constitutes a firm ground for withdrawing the license to function.

Supervision and support

Although the deacons of the ancient church were often the chief aides of their bishops, in the modern church many deacons seldom get to see or talk with their bishop. Deacons can seek out special occasions to be with the bishop not only in the liturgy, but also in settings which foster mutual knowledge and understanding, One model of such an encounter is found in the diocese of Rhode Island, where Bishop George Hunt takes newly ordained deacons on a tour of Israel. Several bishops take a deacon with them as they go about the diocese to visit parishes. If possible, a deacon and the bishop can sit down once a year to evaluate performance, share opinions, isolate areas of conflict, and set goals. This review can help in the revision of the letter of agreement.

The bishop of Southeast Florida, Calvin O. Schofield, attended the annual retreat of his deacons in July 1989. As they briefly told him their stories, Schofield listened "to the astounding diversity and depth of what our deacons are doing." He concluded that most deacons "responded to the urgent needs of the world around them in ways different from what they had projected for themselves in their statements of ministry."[5] In three other dioceses where the deacons had gathered for one of their regular meetings, the directors asked them to write down a brief account of their ministry. These stories were collected and forwarded to me, and I assume they were also shared among the deacons at the meeting.

But all is not well. It may happen that a bishop who is supportive of deacons retires and is replaced by a bishop who is not. Other bishops want to support their deacons, but are confused about their meaning and functions; some frequently change their minds, or are fuzzy about resolving conflicts. Some dioceses lose track of their deacons completely, while others never bother to ask. My contact person in one diocese with a large number of deacons reported, "No one at the diocesan house knows what the deacons are doing!" In a midwestern diocese with a large number of deacons the program director responded, "No single person has this information and there is no one to take on the task of getting it." Another program director reported that more than half of the almost twenty deacons are either inactive, unknown, or do not work with the poor. In many dioceses deacons who should be the bishop's eyes and ears have been allowed to slip into the shadows and become invisible. Partly this is the fault of deacons who forget their ordination vow to "be guided by the pastoral direction and leadership" of the bishop, but the main responsibility belongs to their bishops.

Parish-based deacons should consult frequently with the priest in order to monitor their effectiveness, review assignments, and evaluate spiritual and professional growth. Just as deacons have a voice (and usually, but not necessarily, a vote) in diocesan convention, they need to have a voice in the parish vestry. The parish that either chose them or consented to their assignment has the right to hear their voice, and the deacons have the duty to speak.

Deacons who work mainly outside the institutional church sometimes come into conflict with their parish priest, who may expect them to help within the parish. At the outset of the assignment, there needs to be clarity about what the deacon's role is to be, and periodically thereafter a review of expectations and changing circumstances.

In the parish, areas of conflict may occur in the liturgy, where deacons and other baptized persons have been granted overlapping roles. Although deacons normally lead the prayers of the people and administer the wine, they should include others in functions which the church finds useful or meaningful. Deacons do not normally function in liturgical roles proper to priests or other persons. Similarly priests do not normally vest as a deacon or act as a deacon in the liturgy (although in the absence of a deacon they may perform diaconal functions).[6]

The parish may clearly set forth the terms involved in a deacon's work, the hours per week, and areas of responsibility. These can be specified in a letter of agreement between deacon and bishop (or a separate letter within the parish). Although there is no absolute standard for such terms, which vary from place to place, parish-based deacons who are otherwise employed commonly work for the church ten or more hours a week without financial remuneration.

Deacons derive most of their support from continuing education events, meetings of deacons and other groups, and the development of spiritual life. Parishes and dioceses should try to include continuing education funds for deacons in their budgets. Some dioceses even require deacons to draw up a plan for continuing education, and a long-range program for diaconal formation might include: participation in ongoing programs for the diaconate (national, provincial, or diocesan); two weeks each year for development of diaconal capability; and sabbatical leave for study, research, and reflection. The letter of agreement may specify leave accumulated at the rate of two to four weeks per year.

Deacons can become members of support groups on several levels: with lay persons, including spouse and family, both in and outside the parish; with other deacons, informally with spouses and formally in meetings, one or two of which should include the bishop; and with presbyters, both socially and formally with the priests of an area, including meetings of the local clericus (clergy of a deanery or convocation).

In some dioceses the summer camp session, lasting several days to a week, is used to satisfy needs of supervision and support. Candidates are integrated into the diaconal community, deacons receive continuing education and mutual support, and the bishop gets to meet with, teach, hear, and worship with the deacons. At an annual retreat of the deacons and candidates of Northern Indiana, for example, a high point of the weekend was the ancient ceremony of washing feet. All removed shoes. In turn, each person sat in a central chair, received foot-washing from someone else, and then knelt before the chair to wash the next person's feet. During this action, a cantor sang a long text based on John 13, to plainchant, and the people responded with a refrain in a folk-like melody. By washing the feet of their brothers and sisters who are servants in Christ, the deacons rehearsed washing the feet of the poor.

The finding, nurture, and care of deacons, then, is a community enterprise. It includes the bishop, who has sworn to guide and strengthen the deacons and all others who minister in the church, and who has a Christian duty to pay them close attention and stir up their ministry. It includes the presbyters, who build up and lead the church in every place and work with deacons and others in a team that supports ministry. Most importantly, it includes vast numbers of Christians who, with the deacons, carry out the great work of mercy, justice, and peace among the poor of the Lord.

ENDNOTES

1. *Diakoneo* 11:3 (May 1989), 8.

2. Ibid., 8-9.

3. In Northern Michigan in 1990, Bishop Thomas K. Ray began to commission, in a single liturgy, "ministry support teams" in small parishes. Each team includes [lay] coordinators of ministry, local priests, and local deacons. See *The Living Church*, 27 May 1990, p. 8.

4. See Ormonde Plater, *The Deacon in the Liturgy* (Boston: National Center for the Diaconate, 1981), and Howard E. Galley, *The Ceremonies of the Eucharist: A Guide to Celebration* (Cambridge, Mass.: Cowley Publications, 1989).

5. "The Bishop's View," *The Net* [diocese of Southeast Florida], Sept. 1989, p. 5.

6. J. Neil Alexander argues that because ordained persons continue as members of previous orders, a priest may vest and serve as a deacon (but not as a "presbyteral deacon," shifting from one order to the other), "A Call to Adventure: Seven Propositions on Ministry," in *This Sacred History: Anglican Reflections for John Booty*, ed. Donald S. Armentrout (Cambridge, Mass.: Cowley Publications, 1990), pp. 27-28. Galley discourages the practice as unfaithful to the prayer book rubrics (BCP, p. 354), although not strictly forbidden by them, p. 28. Also opposed is Byron D. Stuhlman, *Prayer Book Rubrics Expanded* (New York: Church Hymnal Corp., 1987), p. 15.

8

Deacons in the World

I n this chapter, by showing the many ways in which deacons function, I hope to encourage the ministry of the whole church. These stories hold up a mirror image of the great diversity and range of ministries performed by Christian people of all kinds. They reveal what is already taking place, show how deacons model and encourage diaconal ministries for others, and provide a guide for those who call persons for the diaconate, as well as for those who are called.

The following sketches include many deacons in the Episcopal Church. The emphasis is on active deacons and their service in the world, but I include some deacons who have retired and still have valuable ministries, or who work within the institutional structures of the church. Many deacons with a ministry of outreach also visit the sick and shut-in of their parish; many see their ministry as partly in their place of employment, partly in the parish, and partly in other areas of care. There is not space enough to include all the deacons I have researched, so consider these stories a partial tableau of the diaconate as it has evolved and taken shape over the past decade.

People frequently ask for lists of deacons in special areas—AIDS, hospice, addiction, and so forth. To get in touch with any of the following persons, a convenient and accurate source is the directory published by the North American Association for the Diaconate, revised yearly, which contains names and addresses of the deacons in each diocese.

The social ministry of most deacons fits into one or more of the six categories named by Christ in Matthew 25:31-46. When I mention a deacon as serving in one category, I do not mean to exclude other categories. A person who hungers often also is homeless and sick; a person who is homeless often also suffers from a breakdown in family relationships.

I was hungry and you gave me food

Programs to feed the hungry take place on several levels, including diocesan, parish, agency, and ecumenical. Some deacons, such as Jean Olsen of Rhode Island, serve on diocesan hunger task forces. Many work in parish soup kitchens or food pantries (to give two of the most common names). These include Irvin Maranville of Vermont, who operates the Open Door Ministry and soup kitchen for the poor and homeless; Virginia Kirk of Pennsylvania, in charge of a parish program of feeding the hungry in the neighborhood; Jeane Steele of Pittsburgh, who directs Meals-on-Wheels in Monroeville; Susan Harrison of Georgia, who coordinates a daily soup kitchen sponsored by Episcopal churches in Savannah; Kermit Bailey of North Carolina, who directs emergency relief for the Greensboro Urban Ministry and dishes out supper at a night shelter; Beth Thomas of Colorado, who coordinates the Colorado branch of SHARE, a food distribution, self-help, and resource program; and Matthew Janiak of Utah, who sits on the board of Acts 6 soup kitchen.

In an unusual ministry involving much individual initiative, Fred Butler of Michigan drives almost eight hundred miles a week delivering day-old pastries from local bakeries to numerous charities. He also delivers donated items such as clothing and appliances.

Feeding the hungry sometimes seems an endless process. One day, serving food in a soup kitchen, Jim Thompson of Oregon thought, "Same old people. Day after day. Wonder if it does any good?" On Sunday he stood behind the altar rail, serving the wine at the eucharist, and thought, "Same old people. Sunday after Sunday. Wonder if it does any good?"

I was thirsty and you gave me something to drink

In this category, I use thirst metaphorically—as the thirst of the poor for faith, hope, and love. The drink we give them is the living water of the spirit, of the good news, and of the knowledge of truth. We are to give them spiritual, evangelical, and educational support.

Spiritual

Spiritual support includes those who run retreat centers, lead retreats, lead groups, and in general provide spiritual direction. Minka Sprague, professor of New Testament and biblical languages at New York Theological Seminary, gives conferences and retreats throughout the church, and has taught ethics, systematic theology, and New Testament in Sing Sing. Mary Craig Rice of Central Florida lectures to church groups about the relationship between the psychology of Carl Jung, biblical literature, and individual counseling. Vicki Black of Milwaukee is retreat and conference coordinator for DeKoven Center. Helen Mountford of Kansas coordinates retreats for the diocesan Spiritual Development Committee. Marie Webner of Arizona leads retreats as chaplain of the American Province of the Third Order of St. Francis. David Alves of El Camino Real finds his ministry in the work place and home place, leading groups in prayer and Bible study.

Evangelical

Evangelical support emphasizes the spread of the good news, chiefly by word but also by music and other arts. Jerry Meachen of Connecticut is one of several deacons who are organists, choirmasters, and composers. David Hardin of Chicago is host of a weekly ecumenical TV program, "An Hour of Good News," on WTTW in Wilmette. Carol Burgess of Minnesota encourages diaconal ministry at the Union Gospel Mission. William Henwood of Arizona uses his job as a mechanical engineer with a Tucson architectural firm to get in touch with people who have no church home.

Educational

Educational support concentrates on the spread of knowledge of all kinds. Virginia Eklund of Lexington has a teaching ministry coupled with counseling. Cyril White of Southeast Florida teaches education and industrial arts education at Sunset Senior High. Bercry Leas of Michigan, a professional teacher of English, focuses her ministry on Christian education. Andrew Palmer of Oklahoma teaches the functionally illiterate to read in a program of the local library association. In Rio Grande, Nan Collins of El Paso works to develop "Every Member Ministry" by traveling through her region to preach and teach, mentor EFM classes, and teach Christian caregiving, Bible, and discernment of gifts. Betty Fuller of West Texas developed a biblical teaching curriculum for small churches, called "Seedlings," which she sells by mail order. Barbara Riker of Olympia teaches at the diocesan School of Theology.

I was a stranger and you welcomed me

To welcome a stranger is to open one's door to refugees, aliens, and the dispossessed, to ethnic groups who are aliens in their own land, to seamen and migrant workers who are often away from home, and to the lonely who are foreigners in their own community.

Refugees and aliens

In Rhode Island, Ida Johnson coordinates refugee activities for the diocese, while Jean Olsen has been active in resettling Cambodians in Providence. Edith Wilson of Maryland works in the federal immigration program. In Minnesota, Joan Dezhad finds sponsors and does advocacy for refugees for the Lutheran Church, Pat Drake helps her parish with refugee resettlement, and Lyn Lawyer, as diocesan refugee resettlement coordinator, encourages individuals and parishes in the ministry of resettling refugees.

Ethnic groups

John Burr of Rochester helped to bring about the merger of two parishes as a bi-racial congregation in downtown Rochester. Solomon Lee of Chicago aids his Korean people. In South Dakota, nine deacons are of the Lakota tribe and minister to the Lakota people, but all eighteen deacons in the diocese minister to the Indian community. In Northwest Texas, Herb Pijan works with Hispanics seeking American citizenship. Nancy King of Oklahoma is assigned to Hispanic ministry at a downtown parish, where she is responsible for outreach. Among the native deacons of Alaska, Jerry Norton upholds his Eskimo people in the fishing village of Kivalina, and Helen Peters is an Athabascan member of a team of native evangelists, who travel the state teaching the gospel and praying with fellow natives. She has a wide pastoral ministry in her home community of Tanana and works at a hostel for mental health patients in Fairbanks. Montie Slusher writes grants and helps train people for native ministries in the interior and Arctic coast of Alaska. Suzanne Tavernetti of El Camino Real has a cross-cultural ministry in a rural agricultural area. Janet King of Idaho works with migrant and seasonal farm workers. In Navajoland, Yazzie Mason works with his Navajo people. Jim Taylor of Nevada works with regional vicars in exploring the possibilities for Hispanic outreach. Sr. Priscilla Jean Wright, CT, and other sisters of the Community of the Transfiguration help the poor in San Pedro de Macoris in the Dominican Republic.

Seamen

In Southern Virginia, Claude Turner is a full-time chaplain at the International Seamen's House in Norfolk. On weekdays and many Sunday evenings he ministers to merchant sailors coming into the port of Hampton Roads. Linda Moeller of Southeast Florida works with the seamen's chaplaincy in the Port of Fort Lauderdale. Hugh and Millie Cooke of San Joaquin, as "angels" for the Seafarers Ministry, visit ships docking at the Port of Stockton.

The lonely

In New York, Br. Justus Van Houten, SSF, has a history of helping the lonely and isolated. Now working for Trinity Parish, Wall Street, previously he spent two or three nights a week with the San Francisco Night Ministry. Paul Jackson of Central Florida runs a taxi service for people who have no transportation to church. In Southeast Florida, Donald Popilek counsels elderly and retired people, works with youths with drug problems, and counsels cruise ship personnel, and Miriam Pratt ministers to the aging and does group counseling, tutorial, and parenting support for teen-agers and their parents. Mary Bradshaw of Nevada coordinates senior citizen transportation for Lincoln County, the only public transportation in the country, except for Amtrak, which operates in the middle of the night. Virginia Hart and her husband, the cooks and managers at Camp Galilee in Nevada, have an ongoing ministry to casino employees, both having worked in the food end of the gaming industry. Gini is also a professional clown.

I was naked and you gave me clothing

The "naked" are all who are exposed and imperilled, beginning with the homeless, who lack shelter, and including all who are open to the elements: the poor, those who suffer from violence and injustice (for whom we seek peace and justice), those exposed to danger as they keep the peace (the police), those in crisis in the family (youth, elderly, singles, married couples, and men and women in search of new identity), and that most ancient of endangered groups, widows and orphans (these days, primarily the children of separation and divorce).

The homeless

Mary Suroviak of Connecticut is a street minister with Isaiah 58 Ministries. Nancy DuBois of Vermont works on the housing crisis in her town and raises awareness among clergy about community needs. Mary Fera of Albany works in a program of shelter and hospitality for the homeless of Troy. Carol Ann Kerbel of New Jersey runs a crisis ministry, funded jointly by Episcopal and Presbyterian churches, to aid the hungry and homeless in Trenton by offering food, clothing, utilities, transportation, and other help in emergencies. Mary Brown of Pittsburgh works in a street and institution ministry. In Southeast Florida, Lawrence Crary, an attorney, gives legal counsel to the homeless and those with housing needs. Lynn Ramshaw, formerly assistant to the bishop of Southeast Florida for social concerns, helped organize St. Laurence Chapel, a building which provides the homeless with bathrooms, showers, tables and chairs, worship, mail and telephone facilities, and help with paperwork.

Barbara Jean Wagner of Michigan works with the homeless children of alcoholics. Marcia Stackhouse of Colorado is employed by the Denver Emergency Housing Coalition and coordinates the Episcopal Pastoral Center in Denver. Judy Cirves of Milwaukee works at the homeless shelter at Grace Church, Madison, Wisconsin. Carmen Edwards of Minnesota works with the city council in Redwing, particularly in housing, redevelopment, and food shelves. James Brown of Kansas works with housing ministry in Kansas City. Roger Riggsby helps the homeless in El Camino Real. Robert Moore of Hawaii works four days a week for Honolulu's street ministry, Institute for Human Services.

In Oregon, Penny Berktold enables and supports ministries at her parish (St. Mary's, Eugene, where her husband is the rector), works with a parish nursery for homeless children, sits on the board of Mothers Against Drunk Driving, and is the Episcopal chaplain at Lane Community College (working mainly with older students trying to get off the welfare rolls). Jenny Vervynck of San Diego works with the homeless through Faith and Love Ministries, a shelter and soup kitchen.

The poor

Ralph Anderson of Western Massachusetts coordinates a person-to-person community action program for All Saints', Worcester. In Maryland, Dennis Hewitt helps a mission in West Baltimore to evangelize its poverty-stricken community, and Althea Quarles works at a Jubilee center in the Baltimore inner city. Marvin Suit of

Lexington works with illiterate persons in Fleming County, Kentucky. In Michigan, Jennie Farmer works at Habitat for Humanity, and Anne Kramer and Beverly Pruitt minister in outreach to the poor. In Colorado, Sarah Butler directs the Stephen Ministry and senior referral services at St. John's Cathedral, Cindy Irvin directs the Good Samaritan Center in Cortez, David Jones directs Rainbow Life Ministries in Broomfield, Joseph Payne, a lawyer, helps indigent people in court cases, and Kay Wood spends thirty to forty hours a week as director of Ruth House, helping unemployed women over forty learn job skills.

Pamela Dunbar of Northwest Texas is youth advisor and tutor at Casa de Amigos (a Hispanic community center), parish coordinator and deliverer of food for low-income persons outside the parish, and a contact person for families in need. In Utah, Elizabeth Cunningham collects clothing and food for several distribution centers, while Irene Rael is a member of the ecumenical Ministerial Alliance, runs a food pantry for the elderly, and gives financial aid to transients needing shelter, food, or gas.

Those in crisis

Mary Sleeper of Maine has worked as a volunteer with a city hot line program, Diocesan AIDS Task Force, Family Crisis Center, and many people in need of food and shelter. Marilyn Powell of Tennessee is co-leader of the Mid-Cumberland Mountain Ministry, an agency that serves the critical needs of persons in three counties, including housing, family violence, literacy, substance abuse, young people in juvenile court, truckers, prisoners, and emergency food, clothing, and shelter. Sherry Young of Michigan does grief counseling. Sarah Tracy, archdeacon of Northern Indiana, founded St. Margaret House, a day shelter for women in South Bend, Indiana.

Bob Davidson of Colorado directs the Crisis/Information Helpline of Larimer County. Patsy Masterman of Fort Worth works on the staff of the Presbyterian Night Shelter as assistant director of the transitional work program, which teaches job and social skills. In Kansas, Joe Thompson, a Red Cross volunteer for sixty-five years, teaches CPR and first aid; Jim Upton teaches disabled children and is active in the Breakthrough Club of Episcopal Social Services in Wichita, a program to enable people released from mental institutions to adapt to regular life; and Bob Parker is executive director of Episcopal Social Services in Wichita, where he supervises seven paid staff and almost three hundred volunteers, who provide counseling and emergency help, support for the mentally ill, and hot meals.

Two deacons of Northwest Texas help in multiple areas of crisis: Brenda Carpenter visits in hospitals and nursing homes, counsels those in crises (rape, substance abuse, AIDS), works in outreach projects for the aged and needy, and is an emergency room chaplain. Betty Smith is a chaplain with hospice, works with the homeless, coordinates Meals-on-Wheels on weekends, and is a Stephen ministry leader and a suicide crisis volunteer and teacher. Jean Stiles of Arizona coordinates group meetings called HUGS (Healing and Understanding Grief Series), which help people deal with loss and grief.

Dorothy Nakatsuji of Hawaii, who has a background in psychiatric nursing, was formerly spiritual counselor for several women, patient care coordinator with Hospice Hawaii, and informal minister to the dying and their families. She now works in the outreach program at St. Clement's, Macaque. Her ministry has evolved into helping others to discern and develop their own ministries.

Peace and justice

Several deacons deal with justice issues as part of their employment, such as Mac Barnum of Connecticut, who uses his business to consult on ethical management practices, and Eric Dawson of the Virgin Islands, who is an attorney and the commissioner of economic development and agriculture with the government. Pamela Lightsey of Georgia works as a volunteer with the Valdosta DA's office in helping and counseling crime victims. Barbara Armstrong is one of North Carolina's two registered lobbyists at the state General Assembly; she functions as a liaison with legislators on issues of criminal justice, child care, the aging, alcohol, and similar concerns. David Karcher of Southeast Florida, an attorney, provides legal services for the indigent, helps as chaplain to the South Miami Police Department, and is a certified crisis intervenor for emergency personnel.

Bob Herbert of Western North Carolina is a legal guardian in Henderson County. Tom Trimmer of Michigan traveled to Central America in the fall of 1989 as a member of the Episcopal Church delegation of Witness for Peace, in which eighteen persons from eleven dioceses spent a week in Guatemala and two weeks in Nicaragua. In February 1990 he helped monitor the election in Nicaragua. Richard Miller of Northern Indiana is a labor union organizer who seeks justice for workers and thus is seen as an icon of Christ in the work force. Sally Brown of Colorado, on Congresswoman Pat Schroeder's staff, is active in peace, justice, and advocacy. Bob Franken of Colorado helps in youth ministry and the Stephen Ministry and is an advocate for social justice for the handicapped. Gary Snow of South Dakota has a dual role: in his work as an asbestos consultant in schools and offices he often deals with the effect of stress, and he also has a political ministry. Judith Ain of El Camino Real conducts the Emmaus Road Ministry, in which she ministers as chaplain on peace walks and speaks about the gospel call to make peace.

Police

Edward Trafford of Rhode Island is chaplain of the Providence police department. Arthur Scrutchins of Oklahoma helps as a police chaplain, counseling police officers, victims of crime, and the relatives of accident victims. Thomas Minnerly of Spokane, police chaplain for the Spokane County Sheriff's Department, rides an eight-hour shift in a patrol car in a ministry that is focused on officers and victims, as well as training persons in a Stephen program.

Youth and college work

In Connecticut, John Lantz, a professor at the University of Bridgeport, ministers to students in crisis; Katherine Lwebuga-Mukasa is a child advocate consultant; Eleanor Schofield, a public school teacher, volunteers as guidance counselor to disadvantaged children at Sacred Heart-St. Anthony School in Bridgeport; and Carolyn Shears provides counseling for teen-agers through her own business, Hosanna House Ministries. Gail Wheelock is chaplain at Rhode Island College. In Vermont, Catherine Cooke is a university chaplain, and Mary Pratt works with a community action group and is the youth coordinator for the diocese.

Jim Poole of Albany, head of transportation in the Gilbertsville school system, ministers to four hundred young people at Oneonta's Job Corp Center. Anne Reed of Maryland works with drop-out children in the inner city. Mark Rivera of Central Florida directs Anchor House Ministries near Auburndale, a home for about twenty troubled boys, which he founded in 1974. Charles Oglesby of North Carolina is a counselor at North Carolina State University. In Southeast Florida,

Shedrick Gilbert ministers to inner-city boys, and Carroll Mallin is regional director of Florida United Methodist Children's Home. Stewart Stoudemire of Western North Carolina is a leader in the PALS program which pairs troubled youth with caring adults in Hickory. Nancy Copass-Tiederman of Indianapolis is a chaplain at Purdue University, where she mainly counsels graduate students. Thalia Johnson of Michigan recruits, trains, and supports 4-H workers in Lenawee County. Terry Gerry of Milwaukee does youth and campus ministry at the University of Wisconsin in Milwaukee and Marquette University.

Roy Chrisman of Nebraska took some twenty youth to work in Honduras in June 1989. He ministers as a crisis-intervention counselor, youth leader, Cursillo participant, and member of the Christian education commission on the diocese. Nancy Huston of Nebraska spent a year in Honduras as a missionary high school teacher at the Episcopal school in Puerto Cortes on the north coast. Ann Gorrell of Kansas is active in suicide prevention among teen-agers in southeast Kansas. In Oklahoma, Bert Bibens works with troubled adolescents—runaways, drug addicts, pregnancies; Lois Gatchell is a national consultant to organizations and committees concerned with teen-age pregnancy; and Patrick Roarke, a lawyer in Bartlesville, helps as a counselor and advocate for teen-agers in trouble with the law.

In Western Kansas, Joe Withrow and his wife are house parents for children in the process of becoming foster children. Tom Cory of California is a chaplain with the Boy Scouts and Engagement Encounter. Jim Mosier of Eastern Oregon is administrator of Juvenile Court Resources, Inc., which provides services for youths whose lives are affected by the juvenile justice system; he directs twenty programs, including drug and alcohol abuse, foster care, and sexual injury. In Hawaii, Eleanor Akina works as a child psychiatrist, primarily with the Windward Counseling Center of the State Department of Health, and Charleen Crean is lower school chaplain at Iolani School. Carol Dodson of Idaho works with the state health and welfare department in child protection.

Elderly

Jackie Merrill of Maine has a ministry with the geriatric patients of her employer, an ophthalmologist. Joyce Maranville of Vermont organizes volunteers to read to the elderly in nursing homes. Humbert Thomas of Western Massachusetts, a retired ice cream parlor owner, works as a paid advocate for the elderly, helping them through the bureaucratic maze of Social Security and Medicaid. Virginia Thomas of Pennsylvania, now retired in Vermont, began the Dolphin program in the early 1980s by gathering volunteers from several denominations to visit and become friends with lonely people. In Pittsburgh, several deacons work in the Dolphin ministry: Ann Staples (coordinator), Ruth Manson, and Joanne Hetrick. Nancy Wood is ECW chaplain of Southern Virginia and visits the elderly.

In Southeast Florida, Denise Hudpeth works as director of social activities at Bishop Gray Center, Lake Worth; Reimar Schacht directs a social club for senior citizens; and SuzeAnne Silla ministers to the elderly, sick, and shut-in and works for hospice. Peg Ferguson of Western North Carolina works with the elderly in a retirement home. Martha Ponader leads a team working with the elderly in the neighborhood surrounding St. Alban's, Indianapolis. Hubert Billington of Colorado works for the aging and retired, helps provide respite care for those with chronically ill family members, and volunteers at the Carnegie Library. Jole Hart of Wyoming is the diocesan designee for the Episcopal Society for

Ministry to the Aging. Patricia Walker of Olympia works for the Social Security administration.

Single persons and families

Dorothy Faison of Pennsylvania organized and leads the Delaware Deanery Singles club, and she will expand singles clubs into other deaneries. Paul Pickens of Rhode Island counsels and refers in family, marital, vocational, and pastoral care matters; he is also a member of the social action committee of the Rhode Island Council of Churches. Jean Ann Eitel of Southeast Florida ministers to broken families and children in need. In Colorado, Wayne Ewing, a psychotherapist, has diocesan responsibilities for family life, and Patrick Griffin works as a pastoral counselor and is involved at the University of Denver in marriage and family therapy. Marlene Ceynar of Minnesota coordinates Volunteers Working Together, a family services activity in Wadena. Bob Snow of Nebraska and his wife lead marriage encounter weekends. In Oklahoma, Gayle Bridges is a pastoral psychologist at the Samaritan Center for Counseling and Psychotherapy, a non-profit ecumenical agency helping children, individuals, and families in the Oklahoma City area, and Gary Templeton facilitates a group called Co-Dependents Anonymous and wants to start a dialogue group for men exploring the meaning of manhood.

Women

Virginia Poole of North Carolina works at a women's center in Raleigh. Eleanor Hill, archdeacon of Oklahoma, directs Resonance, an ecumenical counseling agency for women in transition or other stress (using women volunteers). Bryan Duffty of El Camino Real has established Genesis House for the care of unwed mothers.

I was sick and you took care of me

Professional chaplains

At least six deacons are employed as full-time professional chaplains. Timothy Mylott of Western Massachusetts works as the chief chaplain at the Belchertown hospital for the mentally retarded. In Kentucky, Georgine Buckwalter of Kentucky is employed as chaplain at Westminster Terrace Retirement Nursing Home in Louisville, and Helen Jones is chaplain at Norton's Infirmary, an Episcopal hospital. JoAnn Garma of Louisiana (a former professional prison chaplain) is the chaplain at Children's Hospital, New Orleans, where she supervises a CPE program. Martha Bradley of Springfield is chaplain at St. John's Hospital.

Connie Hartquist of California is one of several full-time chaplains at San Francisco General Hospital and an authority on ministry to AIDS patients. In the hospital she trains and leads an ecumenical group of volunteer "assistant chaplains," who visit patients on the margin of society: the homeless, refugees and immigrants, IV drug abusers, alcoholics, persons with AIDS, trauma victims (injured through auto or motorcycle accidents, stabbing, sexual assault, or homicide attempts), and the elderly poor. In 1988 Hartquist spent six weeks in London and Stockholm conducting AIDS workshops.

Professional health care workers

Others deacons minister to the sick as part of, or in connection with, their professional employment (or former employment) as doctors, nurses, directors, or other workers in health care. Three are in Connecticut: Fran Bedell works as an oncology nurse at Uncas-on-Thames Hospital in New London; Carolyn Garside is employed as recreation director at Cheshire Convalescent

Home; and Jan Jaeger works as night manager at Avery Heights, a retirement health care facility, and is also a counselor and assistant chaplain at Church Home of Hartford. Bruce Alexander of Maine manages a nursing home in Waterville. Catherine Cooke of Vermont is a registered nurse, as is Doug Alamillo of Albany. Cora Booth of Albany runs hospice for lower Essex County; she trains volunteers and gives them support. Clara Gillies of Western New York is in charge of the physical needs of Refuge House, which provides shelter for six to ten homeless men with AIDS; she counsels them and their families. Jon Shematek of Maryland, a pediatrician, works for hospice, while Gibson Wells, a retired pediatrician, is chaplain coordinator for the diocese.

Linda Bronsted of Central Florida, a former pediatrics nurse, is a chaplain on the pediatrics floor of Orlando Regional Medical Center. In Kentucky, Lee Maglinger is a mental health counselor with the Kentucky Department of Human Services, and Eva Markham, a psychologist, helps Madisonville through counseling and teaching. In Lexington, Allen Dawson is a medical doctor whose ministry includes work with the elderly, and Orville Stein, a medical doctor, serves at cost-adjusted and free clinics in eastern Kentucky. John Earl of Western North Carolina is a physician who integrates ministry into his medical practice and offers counseling without fee to the disadvantaged in Hickory. Judy Spruhan of Chicago is a visiting nurse.

In Eau Claire, Larry Edson helps the sick as part of his job as chief of staff at Victory Memorial Hospital in Stanley, Wisconsin, and James Wilson is a family doctor and chaplain in the Order of St. Luke. Rose Ann Smith of Northwest Texas, a family nurse practitioner, is director of nursing education at an acute care facility in Amarillo; she also ministers to the aged and those with AIDS. In Western Kansas, Robert Long works in

Pakistan as a physician in a church-sponsored program for the poor, and Don Martin is employed at Golden Plains West, a residential center in Goodland for the mentally retarded and handicapped. In California, Anne Vellom, a licensed nurse midwife, also functions as a hospice chaplain, and her husband Skip works for Step One, a rehab center; Stan Coppel, a police chaplain in South San Francisco, is administrator of Hill Haven Convalescent Homes in Oakland. In Hawaii, John Kim is an interpreter at Queen's Hospital, and Linda Neal is an employee in a hospital addiction program.

Hospital chaplains

Many deacons are chaplains in hospitals, retirement homes, and similar institutions on a part-time or volunteer basis. A few receive partial payment, at least for expenses, but most are non-stipendiary.

In Connecticut, Richard Beattie is a chaplain in the rehabilitation unit of the Yale-New Haven Hospital, and Janet Wight visits out-of-town Episcopalians in two New Haven hospitals. In Maine, Tom Benson is Episcopal chaplain in the Bangor hospitals, and Audrey Delafield at the Maine Medical Center in Portland. Rhode Island chaplains include Austin Almon at the Pawtucket Institute for Health Services and Ida Johnson at the Rhode Island Medical Center. In Vermont, Polly Bove works as chaplain in a Burlington hospital, and Beverly St. Germain coordinates Episcopal clergy visits in several hospitals.

Tom Williams of Rochester is a chaplain at Schuyler County Hospital. Western New York chaplains include John Derbyshire at Children's Hospital, Paulette Hill at Kenmore Mercy Hospital, Edith Patterson at Millard Fillmore Hospital, and Richard Molison at Sisters Hospital. Frank Dawson of Maryland is chaplain at Fairhaven Hospital. In Pennsylvania, Edgar Chatman-Royce helps with the admission of new patients at Downing Town Hospital.

In Florida, Jay Lauer coordinates ministry in the major medical centers of Gainesville, and Jim Weber visits in three Tallahassee hospitals. North Carolina chaplains include Betty Grant in Duke University Medical Center and Delia Higgins in High Point Regional Hospital. In Southeast Florida, Louise Baker has a daily ministry at the Miami Heart Institute, and Joan Lois Noetzel is chaplain at Martin Memorial Hospital. In Southwest Florida, Wilkin Fisher is chaplain at Bayfront Medical Center in St. Petersburg. David Nard of Western North Carolina is a chaplain at St. Joseph's Hospital in Asheville.

John Thompson of Milwaukee works for Episcopal City Mission, a hospital chaplaincy in Madison, Wisconsin. In Northern Indiana, Arthur Mattox and his wife help as EMT volunteers in a large rural area. In Springfield, Sheila Cooprider is chaplain at St. Louis University Hospital, and Thomas Langford visits Episcopal patients at Memorial Hospital in Springfield.

Minnesota chaplains include Jed Harris at the Mayo Clinic. Mary Husby of South Dakota calls on out-of-town Episcopalians in Sioux Falls hospitals. John Coleton of Kansas is a chaplain at Baptist Hospital in Kansas City. In Northwest Texas, Ruth Jones coordinates volunteers at Lubbock General Hospital where she also is a chaplain and liaison between chaplains and patients, and Herb Pijan works as a relief chaplain at two hospitals. Bill Saak of Oklahoma is a chaplain in Oklahoma City hospitals. In West Missouri, Chari Mynatt helps as on-call chaplain at two local hospitals, and Edith Temple is reserve chaplain at Research Medical Center.

Betty Lou Thompson of Alaska visits patients in the Native Health Service Hospital in Anchorage and other facilities. Ken Pitcher of Arizona visits in five hospitals in the Sun City area. Harold Gillespie of Eastern Oregon visits at St. Charles Medical Center in Bend. Douglas Brinkworth of El Camino Real helps as chaplain two nights a week at Good Samaritan Hospital in San Jose. In Idaho, Milt Cram and John Farmer visit in the Caldwell Hospital. Mary Drew coordinates hospital chaplaincy for the diocese of Olympia. In San Diego, Frank Urmy is a chaplain in two hospitals and a mortuary. Ann English of Spokane works in hospital ministry with the Tri-City Chaplaincy and is a chaplain at St. Mary's Medical Center in Walla Walla, Washington. Elizabeth Cunningham of Utah visits at the University of Utah Medical Center and is a chaplain at the VA Medical Center.

Nursing home visitors

Many deacons help as chaplains or visit the elderly and long-term sick in nursing homes, rest homes, retirement homes, and convalescent facilities.

In Maine, Maurice Allaire is Episcopal chaplain to patients in Portland area nursing homes, and Mary Sleeper concentrates on nursing home residents who have outlived family and community ties. In Rhode Island, Bob Field is chaplain at the Rhode Island Veterans' Home; Jean Hickox visits nursing homes and day-care centers; and Betsy Lesieur is chaplain at Hallworth House in Providence.

Barbara Gerardi of Long Island works as a chaplain in a nursing home. Mary Martha Solbak of Central Pennsylvania works full-time for her parish, visiting the elderly at home and in eighteen nursing homes and supervising visitors. Nancy Foote, archdeacon of Maryland, helps cathedral parishioners visit the sick and shut-in.

Bill Jefferson of Maryland visits the elderly in nursing homes. In Pennsylvania, Rena Graves visits in nursing homes and visits and cares for many elderly in their homes in West Philadelphia, and Dorothy Jessup teaches baptismal classes and visits in hospitals and nursing homes. Pat Lyle of Louisiana leads a team from her parish who visit in several nursing homes in Baton Rouge.

In California, Arlinda Cosby is director of Episcopal Convalescent Home Ministry in the East Bay; Will Madden visits convalescent homes; Tammy Sparks counsels in her parish and visits convalescent homes for the deanery; and Marylou Taylor is an assistant chaplain in school and convalescent homes. Lawrence Barnett of Eastern Oregon visits and leads worship in El Zora Manor nursing home. In Spokane, Marj Denniston helps as chaplain of Rockwood Manor retirement center, as a pastoral counselor at her parish, and as a trainer with the Stephen ministry. Matthew Janiak of Utah visits in hospitals and nursing homes, and is a volunteer at a diocesan apartment complex for the elderly and disabled.

Specialty: AIDS

The national concern with HIV infection and the AIDS pandemic has caused several deacons to join this ministry. Mac Barnum of Connecticut is a counselor with AIDS patients and families at the McKinney Residence in Stamford. Christopher Sims of Maine is co-chair of the AIDS Task Force and counsels people with AIDS and alcohol problems. Lynne McNulty of Rochester and her husband Brian, a Roman Catholic deacon, have a ministry as an ecumenical deacon couple. After a nine-month chaplain residency CPE program, she began a two-bed hospice, Elisha House, for people with AIDS. Dudley Lippitt of Georgia coordinates pastoral ministries for her Albany parish and ministers to AIDS victims in a prison. Joan Marshall of Western North Carolina is a prime mover in the social ministry endeavors of the diocese and shepherds an AIDS support group in Asheville.

Jerry Germaine of Chicago, who visits a nursing home in Wauconda, also ministers to AIDS victims. Gloria Taylor of Northern Indiana, whose son Lance suffers from AIDS, is the AIDS program coordinator for the diocese. She works with people with AIDS to establish support groups, including a group with prostitutes who have contracted AIDS from their partners. George von Hassell of Northwest Texas (a former Lutheran deacon), after training for twelve weeks at San Francisco General Hospital under the supervision of Connie Hartquist, formed a hospice program to serve three towns and helped establish a "safe house" for AIDS patients. He also speaks to community groups about AIDS, conducts a support group for Hispanics with AIDS, and visits at a federal prison.

Specialty: Hospice

Some deacons support the dying and their families in hospice programs. Margaretta Brown of Connecticut is a member of the chaplaincy team for the Regional Hospice Network. Susan Mueller of Milwaukee visits in hospitals and nursing homes and is a long-time volunteer with the Madison Hospice Center. Alma Simpson of Minnesota works in a local hospice program and senior citizen home and does respite care for persons with AIDS. In Oklahoma, Barbara LaBarre serves in hospice at St. Francis Hospital in Tulsa and is active in an agency that trains people over sixty-five to be companions to aging and home-bound persons. In Rio Grande, Owen Kunkle coordinates volunteers, bereavement, and pastoral care at the Santa Fe hospice, and Kathleene McNellis extends Christian education to the El Paso hospice. In Idaho, Richard Green and Rick Harvey work with hospice with the Mountain States Tumor Institute in Boise.

Specialty: Alcohol and drug abuse

Some deacons work with the victims of substance abuse. Judy Kipnis of Connecticut is a chaplain in the detox unit of Danbury Hospital. In Milwaukee, Judy Cirves chairs the diocesan commission on alcohol and other drug abuse, which trains clergy and assists in interventions, while Thomas Winslow sits on the diocesan commission on alcoholism and coordinates a program to treat chemically dependent professionals at the Milwaukee Psychiatric Hospital. Arthur Mattox of Northern Indiana helps those with chemical (especially alcohol) addiction. Shirley Ellingboe of Kansas chairs the diocesan Alcoholism Commission and is active in CODA, AA, Al-Anon, and crisis counseling associated with drug and alcohol abuse.

Greg Sinclair of Northwest Texas is an addiction counselor in a non-profit recovery center, a junior college instructor in drug and alcohol counseling, visits in jail, and counsels through the church to indigent abusers. Alys Lisle of Rio Grande is spiritual director of a treatment facility where she works with alcoholics, drug addicts, and incest victims. Sylvia Hedlund of San Joaquin and her husband are members of the bishop's advisory committee on alcohol and drug abuse. She is working on her doctoral dissertation, "Deacons as Nurturers of Lay Ministry." Barbara Novak of Spokane, a classical musician, works with those suffering from drug addiction.

Specialty: Handicapped

Many deacons work with the blind, deaf, retarded, and other disabled persons. Donna Kingman of Maine formerly ministered in New Hampshire with deaf children and adults in four schools. In Rhode Island, Iris Mello helped to start a neuro-surgery support group, and Janet Broadhead is the Episcopal chaplain at Joseph Ladd Center for the Retarded. Penny Hawkins of Vermont works with the special education of mentally retarded young adults. John Garceau of Albany works with the developmentally disabled. In Western New York, Mother Rita Dugger, CWC, is assistant vicar of Ephphatha Mission of the Deaf. Lawrence Holman of Pennsylvania ministers to the chronically mentally disabled in a half-way residence. Sallie Bird Dunkle of Maryland has begun a program of support groups for the families of newborn handicapped children. Marvin Aycock of North Carolina is a counselor in the community mental health clinic of Albemarle County. Virgilee Ehmer of southeast Florida has developed a new ministry in sign language for work with the deaf.

Robert Taylor of Indiana, who is almost totally deaf, is a social worker who ministers to the hearing-impaired. Sandra Walton of Colorado is employed part-time as a counselor in a home for the chronically mentally ill. Sam Morford of Nebraska has a special interest in care for those permanently handicapped by mental illness. Carol Tookey of Rio Grande works with government, religious, and social groups to provide medical and other services to the handicapped, elderly, developmentally disabled, and AIDS victims. In West Missouri, William Miller sits on the board of the American Mental Health Fund, for which he has established a national network of media volunteers. In California, Roger Edwards, a naval officer, works with the leper colony in Okinawa; Elsa Pressentin ministers to the deaf in two congregations, serves as executive secretary of the Episcopal Council of the Deaf, and communicates with other deaf Episcopalians through the national computer bulletin board, EUGENE.

Specialty: The abused

Betty Lou Wright of Rhode Island directs Lucy's Hearth, a shelter for battered women. Ann Revel of Milwaukee presented a paper on "The Sexual Abuse of Children" at the International Council of Psychologists convention in July 1990 in Tokyo, Japan. Marilyn Bamford of Minnesota works with the Battered Women's Shelter in Duluth. Kit Hall of Eastern Oregon helped found the Central Oregon Battering and Rape Alliance and visits as a chaplain at St. Charles Medical Center in Bend. Jenny Vervynck of San Diego volunteers at a center for battered women.

I was in prison and you visited me

Several deacons minister as chaplains (some as professionals but most as volunteers) in prisons and other institutions for offenders. A few have ministries to those in halfway houses and other release programs. Other deacons are involved in Kairos, a spiritual program for prisoners modeled on Cursillo, in preaching and other evangelical work, and in other ways related to visiting those in prison.

Prison chaplains

In Connecticut, Katherine Lwebuga-Mukasa is a member of the chaplaincy team at Morgan Street Detention Center in Hartford, and James Todd assists as a chaplain in Bridgeport Jail. Bob Adams of Rhode Island is a chaplain at minimum security prisons. Bruce Gillies of Western New York is an assistant chaplain at Collins Correctional facility in Gowanda, and in the prisons he also leads a Kairos program. Mildred Kratovil of Maryland is a chaplain in women's prisons. William Jones of Southern Virginia, part-time chaplain at the State Penitentiary in Richmond, visits on death row. Joe Ryan of Florida visits prisoners at Union Correctional and Florida Correctional, including death rows, for the diocese.

Jack Trembath of Michigan is chaplain and volunteer coordinator at the Macomb County Jail. In Minnesota, Carol Burgess encourages ministry in the correctional chaplaincy, Harold Fait works full time in the State Prison in Sandstone, Jed Harris is a prison chaplain, and Kay Studley is a chaplain at the Duluth City Jail. Janice Bales of Rio Grande is a full-time chaplain at the New Mexico Women's Correctional Facility, a new women's prison. Ray Fox of California started out as Episcopal chaplain for San Mateo County jails where he recruited others into prison ministry. This work has evolved into the Family of St. Dismas, a church for offenders and their families, which he leads.

In Nevada, Bonnie Polley, an unpaid volunteer, works as full-time chaplain at the jail for Clark County (Las Vegas). She visits prisoners and their families and coordinates all religious activities at the huge and complex detention center. She also coordinates jail and prison ministry for the southern part of the diocese. Marilyn Snodgrass of Olympia is employed as a chaplain at the Purdy Correction Center, a state prison for women.

Ex-offender chaplains

In Western New York, Vern Steffenhagen visits in the Niagara County Jail and helps at Hope House, a halfway house for ex-offenders, and Shirley Trail founded and directs Canaan House, an ecumenical residence for released women inmates in Buffalo. Dorothy Lechner of

Central Pennsylvania is vice president of the Transitional Center for Women, a half-way house.

Other prison deacons

Barbara Crampton of Maine manages a house for visitors to the state prison in Thomaston. Jean Brooks of Vermont is involved in prison ministry, ministry to the poor, and legislative advocacy. With the support of the diocese of Central Florida, Frank Costantino began Christian Prison Ministries in Orlando shortly after his release from Florida State Prison in 1973. He was ordained in 1979 and received a full pardon in 1982. Now he trains volunteers to help with the inmate residents and their families. In Georgia, Jim Aton, a dermatologist, visits a prison one afternoon a week to help inmates with skin ailments.

William Arnold of Southeast Florida directs inmate services for PRIDE, a non-profit corporation that manages prison industries, and he also sits on the boards of six other organizations ministering to prisoners and ex-offenders. In Milwaukee, Len Griffin teaches confirmation class in a federal prison and two state prisons, and Reg Scheeler coordinates the Inside-Outside Program, which uses a bus to take inner-city people to visit in the Milwaukee County Correctional Institution. In Colorado, Susan Brady ministers to women in prison through the Kairos program, and Elizabeth Noice conducts worship and Bible study at the Youth Services Detention Center in Grand Junction.

Firmly based on the teachings of Christ, the ministry of deacons responds to the needs of world in the age in which we live. It is also flexible and creative, and it points to ways in which the service of the church, including deacons, may develop in the coming generation.

9

Deacons in the Coming Age

*M*ore than twenty years have passed since John Howe's historic essay on the diaconate sketched the outlines of a restored order of deacons in the Anglican communion. In the year he wrote, 1968, the order of deaconesses in the Episcopal Church was nearing its end, while perpetual deacons had proved inadequate instruments of social compassion. In a world where vast numbers fell victim to sickness, poverty, and strife, and the very fabric of global society had commenced to unravel, the church began to turn its attention to desperate needs outside its institutional walls. In this setting Howe envisioned a diaconate of simple and humble service "in the lower, mundane levels."

The survey in my previous chapter illustrates that Howe's concept of ordained servants of the needy has come to pass in many places, but there have been shifts in emphasis that he did not anticipate, some of which appear to restore aspects of the diaconate prominent in the ancient church. The principal change has been a shift from the deacon as a provider of service to the deacon as promoter of service. A recent letter from a deacon in the diocese of Kansas, Diane Whallon, tells of just such a change:

It seems that we have, for the most part, attracted people to the diaconate who have some active lay ministry—i.e., doers. But where we live out our diaconate is in a leadership capacity, enabling the ministries of others. This is not to say that we don't actually do some ministry (like hospital visiting, etc.), but most of our time and energy is spent in trying to lead others. And what that means is endless committee meetings and trying to nudge people along, a very different form of ministry than what we experienced as lay people. Coming to that realization and making that transition is very difficult, but it is also characteristic of life on the boundary of church and world.

This letter is a good indication of how deacons have evolved from servants in the street to servants in the board room. But deacons do not stand aside and merely observe the street. In what is probably the oldest practice of southern square-dancing, the caller who shouted the dance steps took part in the dancing instead of standing nearby. Deacons who call on angels, earth, and mother church to leap into the air join the leaping. Deacons who encourage active and dirty service step lively in the dust of the dance floor.

Meanings and models in the ancient world

At the beginning of this book, I introduced a cautionary note about translation. Recent scholarship has challenged the currently popular definitions of *diakonia* and its cognates, including the word *diakonos*. An Eastern Orthodox bishop and theologian, Paulos Gregorios, has argued that *diakonia* or service involves not only mercy, justice, and prophecy, but also worship, upbuilding the church, royal priesthood, and prayer and intercession.[1] This broadening of the definition is reflected (although with different findings) in a book by John N. Collins of Australia, a former Roman Catholic priest who teaches religious education. In a study of hundreds of *diakon-*

words used in Greek writings from the late fifth century before Christ to the fourth century of the Christian era, Collins found that ancient sources fail to support the linguistic assumptions many make when they speak of baptized "servants" in a "servant church" and of deacons as particular "servants."[2] The current interpretation of *diakon-* words as referring solely to social care appears to date from the early nineteenth century, when German Lutherans sought to recover the original ministry of deacons and deaconesses as servants of the poor, the sick, neglected children, and prisoners. The interpretation survived, flourished, was recorded in German theological dictionaries in the 1930s, and after World War II surfaced in Germany as part of the rationale for the establishment of the permanent diaconate by the Roman Catholic Church. Along the way, it influenced the understanding of *diakonia*—now usually translated "service" instead of "ministry"—and the restoration of the diaconate in Anglican and other churches.

When early Christians called someone "deacon," however, they may have had more in mind than the service that all Christians are obliged to perform. Collins finds remarkable consistency among pagan, Jewish, and Christian writers of the ancient Greek world, who tended to use words of *diakonia* and its cognates in three related and often overlapping groups of meaning.

First, they used these terms in the sense of "message," to talk about a go-between, mouthpiece, or courier, who travels from one place to another and conveys goods, who carries messages on behalf of persons in high places (sometimes from a god to mortals, and vice versa), who bears the sacred word as a herald, who interprets the words of others, who intervenes on an important mission, who mediates through writing, and who even stirs the emotions of an audience through song.

Second, they used these terms in the sense of "agency," to talk about an agent, instrument, or medium who conducts an operation, acts on behalf of others, carries out the desires or commands of a superior, implements another's plan, performs civic duties and undertakings, who gets done whatever needs to be done, and who functions within the social system like a tutor, butler, major domo, personal secretary, or other important factotum.

Third, they used these terms in the sense of "attendance," to talk about one who attends to a person or household, waits on others, fetches objects and persons, cares for the needs of a guest, and on formal and hence religious occasions bears the wine cup and conducts the feast with decency and taste.[3]

Early Christian writers used *diakon-* words, including eighty places in the New Testament, to talk about Jesus, themselves, and others as spokesmen and emissaries of heaven, emissaries in the church, and others who exercise commissions within Christian communities to act under God, the church, and the Spirit. When early Christians wrote of a "deacon" of the church, they meant an agent in sacred affairs, who worked closely with the bishop, spoke for him, acted for him, and attended him. Even when the context of the agency was care of the needy, they perceived the activity as ministry to the Lord and not as ministry or service to the poor and the widows. This is the church officer exemplified by Laurence, Vincent, Olympias, and others, deacons of the church, serving God through the bishop, just as the Son carries out the Father's work in creation and salvation.

Meanings and models in the coming world

What are we to make of these ancient meanings and models in the late twentieth century? In many places deacons have anticipated the published conclusions of scholarly research by changing or extending their ministry. Often with the support of their bishops, they have shown that they can appropriate the ancient meanings and expand the definitions of "service" and "servants," as we now understand them, without having to replace these useful terms. Like all other changes in the history of ministry, these have responded to the needs of the church and the world. One characteristic of these changes has been an increased emphasis on the spiritual content, the sacred nature, of the ministry of deacons. Another is a renewed closeness between deacons and their bishops as they conduct a mutual *diakonia*. Based on the new directions in which deacons have been moving in the past decade, many of them based on ancient concepts, in the coming age deacons appear ready to minister in at least three areas: as agents of the bishop, as heralds of the word, and as servants of the poor.

Agents of the bishop
In many dioceses of the Episcopal Church, deacons and their bishops are trying to put into practice the ordination statement: "God now calls you to a special ministry of servanthood directly under your bishop." Other churches have equivalent statements. When bishops join their deacons in training sessions and retreats, or take deacons with them on visitations and other travels, deacons have an opportunity to explore and develop this special relationship. As archdeacons and other diocesan officers, as institutional chaplains, or as deputies on special assignments, deacons can act as agents and personal attendants for their bishop. They do this not merely as individuals but as a college of deacons, and the bishop can help them to realize and strengthen their collegiality.

There is a practical reason, based on Scripture, for expanding the ministry of deacons in this direction. Stephen and the other six in Acts 6 were elected and ordained to take over administrative and charitable duties, so that the apostles could devote themselves "to prayer and to serving the word." Thus, in the life of the church as in the liturgy, deacons can serve the assembly by freeing bishops (and priests) for their primary apostolic work, which is prayer, teaching, and preaching.

The next step is to recognize that the diocesan staff, the modern equivalent of the bishop's household, performs diaconal ministry. The principal members of the staff, archdeacons, canons, personal secretaries, administrators, and others, who so often are priests or lay persons, usually function (except in liturgy) as if they were deacons. Should we put them in the appropriate order, or should we restructure the church so that orders are adaptable to current functions? In some dioceses, as we have seen, the bishop has begun to use real deacons in some of these positions.

Because the local congregation is comparable in size and structure to the "parish" or diocese of the first three centuries, a similar expansion might be carried out in the staffs of the cathedral or parishes, especially large ones, where deacons could function as administrators who release the pastor for presiding, building up, and the ministry of the word. The use of deacons in parishes must be approached with caution, however, for the diaconate stands parallel to the presbyterate and involves the freedom to exercise a wider ministry. Language and practices that treat deacons as subalterns under the "supervision" of priests can be misleading and harmful. The primary relationship of deacons is with the bishop, to whom alone, under God, they are subordinate, but as agents, helpers, and co-workers with a direct and personal connection, even when they are deployed in remote places. This distinction should be publicly recognized and acted out in the life of the church, including its liturgy.[4]

Heralds of the word

At the close of the 1989 conference on the diaconate at Kanuga, Edwin F. Hallenbeck offered the participants three images of deacons, two old and one new, which emphasize the functions of deacons as angels, heralds, or messengers. First, like John the Baptist they "go out to speak in the wilderness, in the broken world." Second, deacons are heralds of the kingdom. Not only through what they say but also by their presence in the church and the world, deacons announce the coming of the kingdom of God. Third, they are weavers of opposites—an image derived from the New England mill country where Hallenbeck lives. Like the warp and the woof, the opposite-running threads in weaving, deacons bring disparate elements together. They hang in the tension of city, world, street, and sanctuary.[5]

As heralds deacons announce messages in several directions. One is carrying the word about the world to the church. As the bishop says in the ordination liturgy of the Episcopal Church, deacons are "to interpret to the church the needs, concerns, and hopes of the world." An interpreter is one who carries images, including words, from one place to another, changing them as needed to make sense in the new context. Deacons interpret when they observe the world and report back to the church. Increasingly, they tell the story of special situations in isolated places unknown to most members of the church. They look and listen. They tell the story when they lead intercession, when they speak in convention, when they edit and write and act and mime and draw and sculpt and sing, when they help their bishops to communicate in the age of technology. Deacons interpret to others so that others will pray and try to help.

Another way of interpretation is carrying the word about Christ from the church to the world. Deeds are not enough; ministry must also be verbal. Deacons exercise an evangelical ministry when they bring the good news to the poor, enter into dialogue with the poor about Christ, and reveal to the poor that they are the real presence of Christ. In liturgy the symbol of evangelical ministry is the solemn proclamation of the gospel, a message within the church, to the church, but with implications of announcement to the world.

Deacons also bear the word when they help to spice up churches that, like the Episcopal Church, tend to represent what one observer has called "religion in its mildest form."[6] They are to rescue the church from the drab secularity of our age and restore mystery to faith. Adding another actor, another costume, another mouth, another hand, another foot, another song, another dance. As we recover true service, let us also recover the venerable tradition of song embodied by the poet deacons Ephrem of Edessa, Romanos the Melodist, Alcuin of Tours, and Francis of Assisi. In restoring the diaconate as a serious ministry in often gloomy settings, we sometimes forget that the symbols of the church are playful instruments whereby we rejoice in God. Deacons serve the assembly when they demonstrate that the people of God are many and diverse and enjoy singing and acting before God.

Anything deacons do to stir up the people, nurture their activity, and get them up and moving turns a corpse into a lively body. There is an old tradition of the itinerant minstrel or jongleur, whose practice of carefree song was taken up as a model by renewal movements in the middle ages. The minstrel can be our new image.

Deacons, be minstrels of Christ, who strum tunes of good news for the dancing poor.

Servants of the poor

A recovered emphasis on deacons as agents of the bishop and heralds of the word by no means detracts from their function as servants of the poor. Social care, which fell within the ecclesiastical domain of many early deacons, continues as a legitimate and valuable activity of deacons at the end of the century, as an authentic adaptation of ancient duties. Just as in every age the ministry of the church owes much of its form to ancient tradition, it is also shaped by current needs. With good reason today, most deacons serve the poor, and so long as the world continues to slip and decline into a sad and feeble shape, this service must remain a central function of the diaconate.

As I look over the stories of hundreds of deacons, impressive in their commitment to the poor, I become aware of the expansion and evolution of social care beyond the church walls in response to crisis in the modern world. Deacons in the Episcopal Church no longer typically serve as parish curates. Most deacons exercise ministries of social care among the marginalized members of society, promoting and supporting service among others, and often these ministries occur as part of their professional work. As well as showing mercy for outcasts and the dispossessed, deacons in these ministries have moved into work for justice, peace, ecology, the quality of life, and the very survival of the planet. It is significant that this is the area, beyond the church walls, at home and in the market place, where many other Christians also find their most valuable ministry. And this is the area where bishops have a duty to oversee *diakonia*.

In this sacred work, the best guide remains the Bible and its commands of mercy and justice. When Desmond

Tutu charged the Anglican people of South Africa with service of the dispossessed and oppressed, using images of Christ, he expressed in vivid biblical terms the vision of service that motivates the modern church and the deacons who serve in many and diverse ways:

> When Jesus met a leper, he had compassion and cleansed him; when people were hungry, he had compassion and fed them; when a widow went by to bury her only son, he had compassion on her and raised him from the dead. The compassion of Jesus was not just a passing feeling that made him feel pity but left him wringing his hands. No, compassion moved him to do something to change the situation.

In his speech Tutu taught that people "are of infinite worth because Jesus Christ died for them, and they must be treated not just with respect but with reverence." To treat fellow human beings as less than this "is to spit in the face of God." Tutu then instructed his people:

> A compassionate church will discern the features of its Lord and Master in the drug addict, the homosexual, the hobo, the AIDS patient, the divorcée, the unmarried parent, the hungry, the widow and the orphan, the unemployed, the political prisoner and detainee, the homeless, the oppressed. The compassionate church will, like its Lord and Master, tie a towel round its waist to wash the disciples' feet, because in serving these it knows it is serving him.[7]

As deacons search for new ministries, often based on old models, they continue to wash the feet of the poor, like the Christians of South Africa, and to remind Christians in every land that the worth of human beings is infinite. They do this good work of compassion as messengers, agents, and personal attendants, setting forth on a sacred mission of the highest purpose and greatest urgency.

Remember your many servants, Lord, when you come into your wedding banquet.

ENDNOTES

1. Paulos Mar Gregorios, *The Meaning and Nature of Diakonia* (Geneva: WCC, 1988).

2. John N. Collins, *Diakonia: Reinterpreting the Ancient Sources* (New York and Oxford: Oxford University Press, 1990).

3. The three categories are outlined by Collins, pp. 335-337, and expounded throughout his study.

4. Roman Catholic directions now call for at least three deacons at celebrations presided over by the bishop, "one to proclaim the gospel reading and to minister at the altar, and two to assist the bishop," *Ceremonial of Bishops* (Collegeville, Minn.: The Liturgical Press, 1989), par. 26, p. 24.

5. *Diakoneo* 11:4 (Sept. 1989), 3.

6. See James L. Peacock, "Folk Religion," in *Encyclopedia of Southern Culture*, ed. Charles Reagan Wilson and William Ferris (Chapel Hill and London: University of North Carolina Press, 1989), p. 1285.

7. From the charge of the Archbishop of Cape Town at the Provincial Synod, 31 May 1989, reprinted in *Diocesan Life* [Diocese of Bethlehem]. Sept. 1989.

Appendix

A. Early ordination prayers

Hippolytus, Apostolic Tradition (Rome, c. 215)

God, who created all things and set them in order by
the Word, Father of our Lord Jesus Christ, whom you
sent to serve your will and to show us your desires, give
the Holy Spirit of grace and care and diligence to this
your servant, whom you have chosen to serve your
church and to offer [to bring forward] in your holy of holies the gifts which are offered you by your appointed
high priests, so that serving without blame and with a
pure heart, he may be counted worthy of this high office
and glorify you through your Servant Jesus Christ,
through whom glory and honor to you, the Father and
the Son with the Holy Spirit in the holy church, both
now and to the ages of ages. (Trans. H. Boone Porter)

Apostolic Constitutions (Syria, late fourth century)

For men: God the ruler of all, true and faithful, rich to
all who call on you in truth, awesome in will, wise in
mind, strong and great, hear our prayer, Lord, and
listen to our plea, and show your face on this your
slave, presented to you for the diaconate, and fill him
with spirit and power, as you filled Stephen the martyr
and imitator of the passion of your Christ, and make
him fit to carry out the work of deacon committed to
him, constant, blameless, and irreproachable, that he
may be worthy of higher office, by the mediation of your
only begotten Son, through whom in the Holy Spirit
glory, honor, and veneration to you to the ages. Amen.

For women: God eternal, Father of our Lord Jesus
Christ, creator of man and woman, who filled Miriam
and Deborah and Hannah and Huldah with the Spirit,
who did not shun the birth of your only begotten Son
from a woman, and in the tent of witness and in the

temple set women as keepers of your holy doors, now look down on this your slave, presented for the diaconate, and give her your Holy Spirit, and cleanse her from all stain of flesh and spirit, that she may worthily complete the work committed to her, to your glory and the praise of your Christ, through whom in the Holy Spirit glory and worship to you to the ages. Amen.

B. Lambeth Conference and Anglican Consultative Council

Lambeth 1958: Resolution 88, "The Office of Deacon"

The Conference recommends that each province of the Anglican Communion shall consider whether the office of Deacon shall be restored to its primitive place as a distinctive order in the Church, instead of being regarded as a probationary period for the priesthood.

Lambeth 1968: Resolution 32, "The Diaconate"

The Conference recommends:

(a) That the diaconate, combining service of others with liturgical functions, be open to (i) men and women remaining in secular occupations; (ii) full-time church workers; (iii) those selected for the priesthood.

(b) That Ordinals should, where necessary, be revised (i) to take account of the new role envisaged for the diaconate; (ii) by the removal of reference to the diaconate as "an inferior office"; (iii) by emphasis upon the continuing element of *diakonia* in the ministry of bishops and priests.

(c) That those made deaconesses by laying on of hands with appropriate prayers be declared to be within the diaconate.

(d) That appropriate canonical legislation be enacted by provinces and regional Churches to provide for those already ordained deaconesses.

ACC-3 (1976): Conclusion of report on the diaconate

We appreciate Lambeth's concern to bring the serving or diaconal ministry of the Church more fully within the worshipping and liturgical functions of the whole community. We do not think that the making of deacons on a wider scale than hitherto would cause the laity to feel themselves to be released from responsibility to serve as well as to worship. We would therefore see the Diaconate conferred upon men and women who are deeply committed to Christ within the Church, and who are performing a caring and serving ministry in the world in the name of the Church, or who are carrying out a pastoral ministry in the Church.

ACC-3 (1976): Resolution 10, "The Diaconate"

The Council advises:

(a) that the use of the Diaconate as a period of preparation for the priesthood be retained; and that every church should review its practice to ensure that this period is one of continued training and further testing of vocation; but that it is not to be regarded as necessarily leading to the priesthood;

(b) that the churches, and particularly the laity, be invited to examine the concept of the Diaconate as an Order to which lay people serving the Church, or serving in the name of the Church, could also be admitted, to express and convey the authority of the Church in their service. And, in this consideration, to take into account Resolution 32 of Lambeth 1968, and Bishop John Howe's article on the Diaconate written in preparation for that meeting of Lambeth. This study should include the status of deacons in Synods.

A Select Bibliography

Anglican Church of Canada, General Synod, Committee on Ministry. *A Plan to Restore the Diaconate in the Anglican Church of Canada.* Toronto: Anglican Church of Canada, 1989.

Barnett, James Monroe. *The Diaconate: A Full and Equal Order.* New York: Seabury Press, 1981.

Bishops' Committee on the Permanent Diaconate. *Permanent Deacons in the United States: Guidelines on Their Formation and Ministry.* 1984 Revision. Washington, D.C.: United States Catholic Conference, 1985.

Booty, John E. *The Servant Church: Diaconal Ministry and the Episcopal Church.* Wilton, Conn.: Morehouse-Barlow, 1982.

Borgeson, Josephine, and Lynne Wilson, eds. *Reshaping Ministry: Essays in Memory of Wesley Frensdorff.* Arvada, Colo.: Jethro Publications, 1990.

Church of England, Bishop of Portsmouth [Timothy Bavin]. *Deacons in the Ministry of the Church: A Report to the House of Bishops of the General Synod of the Church of England.* GS 802. London: Church House Publishing, 1988.

Collins, John N. *Diakonia: Reinterpreting the Ancient Sources.* New York and Oxford: Oxford University Press, 1990.

Deacon Digest. Edited by James M. Alt. Green Bay, Wis.: Alt Publishing Co., 1984-.

Diakoneo. Edited by Ormonde Plater. Newsletter of the North American Association for the Diaconate, New Orleans, 1978-.

Directory of Deacons. Providence, R.I.: North American Association for the Diaconate, 1990.

Distinctive Diaconate News. Edited by Sr. Teresa, CSA. Newsletter of Distinctive Diaconate, London, 1981-.

Distinctive Diaconate Studies. Edited by Sr. Teresa, CSA. Occasional papers of Distinctive Diaconate, London, 1981-.

Episcopal Church, Office of Ministry Development. *Signs of Service*. Videotape. New York: Episcopal Church, 1990.

Gregorios, Paulos. *The Meaning and Nature of Diakonia*. Geneva: WCC, 1988.

Halton, Thomas, and Joseph P. Williman, ed. *Diakonia: Studies in Honor of Robert T. Meyer*. Washington, D.C.: Catholic University of America Press, 1986.

Liturgy: Diakonia. Journal of the Liturgical Conference 2:4 (Fall 1982).

McCaslin, Patrick, and Michael G. Lawler. *Sacrament of Service: A Vision of the Permanent Diaconate Today*. New York: Paulist Press, 1986.

Mullan, David S. *Diakonia and the Moa*. Auckland, New Zealand: Methodist Theological College, 1984.

Piccard, Kathryn A. *Research on Women Deacon Saints: An Introduction with Annotated Bibliography*. 2d ed. Cambridge, Mass.: Harvard Divinity School, 1983.

Plater, Ormonde. *The Deacon in the Liturgy*. Boston: National Center for the Diaconate, 1981.

Shugrue, Timothy J. *Service Ministry of the Deacon*. Washington, D.C.: United States Catholic Conference, 1988.

Sr. Teresa, CSA. *Women in the Diaconate*. Distinctive Diaconate Studies 23. London: Community of St. Andrew, 1983-86.

Br. Victor, SSF. *The Servant Leader: impressions of deacons in the USA*. ACCM Occasional Paper 23. London: Advisory Council for the Church's Ministry, 1987.

White, Alison, and Di Williams. *Deacons at Your Service*. Grove Pastoral Series 33. Bramcote, Notts.: Grove Books, 1987.

For other works on *diakonia* and deacons, consult the bibliographies issued periodically by the North American Association for the Diaconate (271 N. Main St., Providence, RI 02903) and by Distinctive Diaconate (2 Tavistock Rd., London W11 1BA).

Index

Scriptural Index